GET ACTIVE

Reimagining Learning Spaces
for Student Success

Dale Basye

Peggy Grant

Stefanie Hausman

Tod Johnston

International Society for Technology in Education
EUGENE, OREGON • ARLINGTON, VIRGINIA

Get Active
Reimagining Learning Spaces for Student Success
Dale Basye, Peggy Grant, Stefanie Hausman, and Tod Johnston

© 2015 International Society for Technology in Education

Editor: *Emily Reed*
Director of Strategy, Clarity Innovations, Inc.: *Steve Burt*
Copy Editor: *Mike Van Mantgem*
Indexer: *Wendy Allex*
Book Design and Production: *Ryan Scheife*

First Edition
ISBN: 978-1-56484-365-4

Printed in the United States of America

ISTE® is a registered trademark of the International Society for Technology in Education.

ABOUT ISTE

The International Society for Technology in Education (ISTE) is the premier nonprofit organization serving educators and education leaders committed to empowering connected learners in a connected world. ISTE serves more than 100,000 education stakeholders throughout the world.

ISTE's innovative offerings include the ISTE Conference & Expo, one of the biggest, most comprehensive ed tech events in the world—as well as the widely adopted ISTE Standards for learning, teaching and leading in the digital age and a robust suite of professional learning resources, including webinars, online courses, consulting services for schools and districts, books, and peer-reviewed journals and publications. Visit iste.org to learn more.

ABOUT THE AUTHORS

Dale Basye is an award-winning writer with more than 20 years of experience developing multimedia experiences for children. He is co-author of *Personalized Learning: A Guide for Engaging Students with Technology* as well as the author of the *Circles of Heck* series.

Peggy Grant is a senior content developer for Clarity Innovations. She taught junior high English and reading before earning her PhD in literacy education. She is co-author of *Personalized Learning: A Guide for Engaging Students with Technology*.

Stefanie Hausman has been a classroom teacher, a teacher coach, a teacher trainer, an education writer, and is currently the Content Manager at Clarity Innovations, where she leads a team of writers dedicated to improving teaching and learning by focusing on the intersection of technology and instruction.

Tod Johnston, a classroom teacher for ten years, focused on creating flexible and student-centered learning experiences for elementary and middle school students both in the United States and abroad. He now uses his classroom expertise as a Content Developer for Clarity Innovations.

ACKNOWLEDGMENTS

We would like to thank our contributing authors, Donna Teuber, Technology Integration Team Leader for South Carolina's Richland School District Two, and David Jakes, ed tech leader and blogger, for their invaluable insights.

We also would like to express our gratitude to Steelcase Education and Intel Corporation for funding this project.

Finally, our thanks go out to all the educators, students, designers, architects, and community members who work every day to create learning environments that educate and inspire.

CONTENTS

FOREWORD

You are about to go on an adventure.

In your hands is a ticket to understanding the power of an active learning space. These are places that help students develop the skills they need in the digital age—communication, collaboration, creativity, and critical thinking—and where they become actively involved in the learning process.

As someone who spends his days talking with students, faculty and educators while visiting schools, colleges and universities and, I assure you these are trips worth taking. I am confident you too would be inspired and energized by the places and people you meet. And you'll meet some of them in this book.

People like Pamela Kennedy, a one-time illustrator and stay-at-home mom, who now teaches in Room 17, an active classroom she helped design in Portland, Oregon. The third graders in her class also helped customize their own learning experiences. That's right, third graders.

You'll meet Stacey Roshan, a high school teacher who successfully flipped her calculus class, a notoriously difficult subject to learn. And you'll meet administrators like Anthony Saba at The Academy, a college-prep school for foster, underserved and community teens. This school has a 97% attendance record thanks in part to the learning spaces that attract kids and help them learn.

You'll tour the Design39Campus, a public school in San Diego where students learn in "studios" with "learning experience designers." The staff has an audacious goal: to change education for students all over the world. Read their amazing story and you may want to join their effort.

Elsewhere in this book you'll encounter learning spaces that expand the idea of the third teacher—the classroom—into the digital realm. You will also learn how involving students in their own education transforms a learning space into a learning experience, and you will explore useful strategies and tactics to help you revolutionize your own learning spaces.

This is a rough guide to the territory with reports from the frontiers of new learning spaces by the people who have spent time there. It's also a workbook to help you take the journey. But it's not just about space. I believe, as so many other educators do, that technology, pedagogy, or space alone is not the answer. Pedagogy as the driver, supported by space and technology, all working together, empower teachers to be their most effective and students their most engaged and successful.

Active learning spaces have been shown to help improve student success, and they're realitvely easy to implement. The emphasis on space comes from what we observe in the classrooms in schools around the world: too many remain single-purpose spaces that only work well for passive teaching methods developed over a century ago. They don't support active learning. Even teachers who embrace active learning pedagogies and who know how to integrate technology into the curriculum are handcuffed by ineffective learning environments: classrooms that don't support communication and collaboration; chairs too big and heavy for students to move; desks and tables that hinder group work, mentoring, information sharing, and content creation. The people featured in this book describe how they have changed their spaces—and how you can, too.

How far you go and how much you get involved depends on how you use this book. You can do any or all of the following:

1. Consider this book to be an *overview* of some exciting new learning spaces and pedagogies. A good use, but one that only mines part of the rich content here.

2. Use this book as a *study guide* that examines the thinking behind new learning spaces, how people planned and designed them, and how you might do the same. A useful journey, perhaps as part of research and planning for reimagining your own classroom or local school.

3. Actually set foot in new territory, a more responsive learning environment. This book can be a "starting point" to places you've always wanted to go as a teacher, school leader, or involved citizen.

Explore this book. Complete the "Your Turn" sections, which are workbook exercises designed to help you assess your own situation and apply solutions. Visit the sites listed in the book to learn more about the learning spaces featured here.

This book is a trip that can take your class to places you never imagined.

—Sean Corcorran
General Manager
Steelcase Education

INTRODUCTION

One of the primary goals educators are tasked with today is to help students become college ready and—more importantly—*career* ready. If you look at modern workspaces, not just in the high-tech industries but most everywhere, you will see that workers are collaborating and connecting across every possible boundary, and with increasing frequency and urgency. Our digital-age workforce relies on dynamic and flexible teams composed of individuals who possess critical thinking skills. Active learning spaces are part of a movement to help today's students become ready for such workplaces so they may better serve the communities in which they'll work and live.

Active learning is a practice and philosophy that supports student engagement. It offers students a variety of learning styles and choices so that they can more easily collaborate with one another, nurture their innate curiosity and creativity, and ultimately succeed. It enables them to go deeper into their education and become immersed in more meaningful learning experiences. Active learning spaces promote student choice, allow for flexibility, and provide profound opportunities to bring the outside world into a student's learning. These spaces also push learning *beyond* the walls of the classroom through blended, flipped, and online learning approaches. It represents a paradigm shift for how we think about learning in school as well as out of school.

This type of multi-disciplined flexibility is, unfortunately, not necessarily a part of the normal skill set that the traditional learning experience instills in students. But it is vital that they learn this way.

Students who become well versed in active learning—earning them the capabilities that colleges, vocational schools, and the workforce demand—will be far more successful than those who are educated in traditional classrooms. It's not that some students can't succeed in a traditional learning environment. Many have. But a more modern, smartly designed learning space offers *more* flexibility and *more* choice to engage students *more* deeply in the process of their own education, thus allowing for *more* adaptable personalized learning approaches that help students to achieve, well . . . *more.*

As schools invest in modernizing their systems, they have to look more holistically in regard to how they design learning environments (both the physical and the blended), where they spend their money, and how they focus on increasing student engagement and achievement. To have a facilities person strictly focusing on space, an IT person strictly focusing on blended space...this doesn't make sense anymore.

It's important to have a variety of skills and expertise at your work table, so make sure that your decision-makers are "all-in" when establishing these new, powerful places of learning. This means you must include leaders in finance, operations, facilities, leadership, instruction, and IT. This book is designed to support multiple stakeholders across *all* team efforts, across *all* boundaries, so that they may create multifaceted plans to help modernize schools—whatever it takes to keep students learning and growing.

Expectations of schools, educators, and students have never been higher. These expectations demand the fostering of new digital-age skills such as literacy, collaboration, and problem solving. It's not just about having education in the classroom becoming more relevant to the outside world: it's about preparing today's students for tomorrow's job skills and helping them to work more efficiently both face-to-face and virtually. Active learning spaces help students build these vital skills while bringing the world into the classroom and allowing for dynamic learning choice.

And creating these vibrant spaces and environments *today* will make classrooms more enduring, adaptable, and accommodating for what learning will look like *tomorrow*. I hope the information and insights provided in this book will help you and your school or district make the important first steps toward bringing the promise of active learning to your students and communities.

—Paige Johnson
Education Strategist, Intel Corporation
ISTE Board of Directors

How to Use This Book

This book is designed to guide thinking about how schools and classrooms can be designed to reflect how students learn and how people work and live in the digital age. Whether you are a classroom teacher, an administrator, a school board member, or an interested parent or community member, you will find information and resources to help you design more responsive, flexible learning spaces that meet the needs of students and teachers.

This book is geared toward the following audiences:

- Teachers who teach in a school environment with a traditional design but would like to make some changes to their classroom arrangement. These individuals will find low-cost, simple suggestions that can help them update their classroom environment.
- Education leaders with progressive pedagogies who feel that their learning spaces are holding back their efforts. These individuals will find strategies for moving an educational community toward more responsive school design.
- School leaders and community members who are planning new buildings or are considering renovating existing schools to accommodate digital-age learners. These individuals will find design suggestions and planning advice to help them update their buildings to reflect how today's students learn best.

The International Society for Technology in Education (ISTE) stands at the forefront of the movement to realize the benefits of technology-rich education and transform how teachers teach and students learn in the modern world. The ISTE Standards for Students, Teachers, and Administrators help guide the digital transition in schools and define best practices in learning, teaching, and leading with technology. As you read, look for these different sets of standards as well as many of ISTE's Essential Conditions for effective technology integrations (2015).

Throughout the book, you will find exercises and activities to help you apply the ideas you are reading about to your current school or classroom, or the school or classroom you would like to create. These exercises include reflections and goal-setting prompts, discussion questions, planning documents, and activities that ask you to investigate various topics related to the learning spaces you have and the spaces you would like to design for the future. Of course, you can complete these activities on your own, but you will find them far more valuable if you partner with a colleague to explore your thinking about what you are reading here.

Overview

Chapter 1, Learning Spaces of the Future, provides an overview of the ways in which schools must be designed in order to meet the needs of students and teachers in this digital age.

Chapter 2, Teaching and Learning in the Digital Age, describes the most effective instructional methods for helping students develop the skills and knowledge they need to be successful, which is accomplished by integrating technology, pedagogy, and learning spaces to create active learning environments.

After establishing the importance of active learning and active learning spaces, the book focuses its attention on the primary learning space in any school: the classroom. In Chapter 3, Reimagining the Classroom, teachers can find practical ideas for designing and furnishing a flexible, student-centered classroom.

In Chapter 4, Redesigning Your Classroom, Donna Teuber, Technology Integration Team Leader for South Carolina's Richland School District Two, empowers teachers to reimagine the classroom. She shares a process for redesigning the classroom and provides helpful tips on involving students and overcoming common challenges.

The most effective learning spaces expand beyond the classroom and utilize spaces throughout a school campus for learning. In Chapter 5, Schools for the Future, the book shifts its focus to the big picture of school design and explores how spaces like school grounds, entryways, and multi-purpose rooms can be transformed for active learning.

Technology removes limits to where and when learning happens. In Chapter 6, Digital Spaces for Learning, ed tech leader and blogger David Jakes explores how virtual spaces extend and enhance learning experiences that are traditionally reserved for the classroom.

Chapter 7, Planning for Active Learning Spaces, describes a process for planning a new or updated school building that supports active learning. This chapter lays out the kinds of decisions that need to be made, who should be involved in the process, and how best to make decisions that will support active learning and grow with the times.

Case Studies

Throughout the book you will read case studies of districts, schools, and classrooms that have used their learning spaces in flexible and innovative ways. These are real-life success stories that illustrate the principles of active learning spaces. In these case studies, you will meet the following educators:

- Kecia Ray, executive director of Learning Technology and Library Services, Metropolitan Nashville Public Schools, Nashville, Tennessee
- Anthony Saba, head of school, The Academy, Santa Ana, California
- Pamela Kennedy, teacher, Meriwether Lewis Elementary School, Portland, Oregon
- Megan Power, teacher and school designer, Design39Campus, Poway, California
- Michael Delp and Jennifer Felke, co-directors, Weidner School of Inquiry, Plymouth, Indiana

 YOUR TURN

Now that you have a general sense about what is in this book, identify how you want to use it. Answer the following questions to help guide your exploration.

1. Why are you interested in active learning spaces?
2. What is your role in creating active learning spaces? An administrator? Teacher? Interested community member?
3. What is the scope of your project? One classroom or a whole school? A repurposing of an existing structure or a brand new building?
4. Who else might be interested in reading this book or discussing learning spaces for the digital age with you?

Identify three goals you hope to accomplish by the end of reading this book.

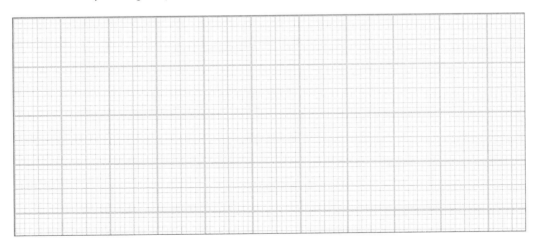

CHAPTER 1

Learning Spaces of the Future

Jake Kahn is a fictional yet realistic 21st-century teen. He is a good student with lots of friends and interests that occupy his out-of-school time. For Jake, there is no such thing as one space for schoolwork and another for personal tasks. He is an anywhere, anytime learner.

Jake's high school is an old building that has been rehabilitated to accommodate flexible learning spaces. Although he takes traditional classes, the lines separating the subject areas are fuzzy, and the physical spaces where he works are blurred and constantly changing.

His teachers take full advantage of the active learning spaces in the school and give Jake considerable control over his own learning. For example, in his English class, for a group project on writing for multimedia, Jake is working with a partner on a video production for the end-of-year banquet for his tennis team. They brainstormed ideas for their video, created a storyboard, and then worked out a script.

Because collaboration is a digital-age skill the school emphasizes, Jake's teacher begins most days by bringing the class together for a short mini-lesson on collaboration skills. On a typical day, after the whole-group presentation, the students rearrange their classroom furniture into small groups to work on their projects. Jake's partner is taking a multimedia production course, so after they have filmed the scenes, they work in the media lab to edit the video and get it ready for feedback from a local media professional. This professional has agreed to meet with them in the evening through Google Hangouts to give them some suggestions.

Jake is excited that he's learning about media production because he has an upcoming collaborative project in his world history class. For that project he plans to suggest they do a video on World War I. His professional mentor suggested some online tutorials that he could look at and an online course he could take for free to refine his video editing skills. Media production brings out his creative side and he really enjoys it, so much so that he's thinking of pursuing it as a possible career path.

At lunch, Jake hangs out with his friends at the café-style lunchroom where he can recharge his laptop and share photos he took on a recent hike with the ecology club. He meets up with some students from his French class, and they make a date to meet at the library the next evening to study for a big test that is coming up later in the week. Jake always likes to make socializing part of his study routine if he can!

Until dinner, Jake plays online games on his Xbox, and then he helps his mother clean up the dishes after he eats. At his usual homework time, he goes to his ergonomically designed study area in his bedroom to work on his world history homework. His history class is designed around the flipped learning model, and his assignment is to watch a video about the causes of World War I and then do some thinking about whether the war could have been avoided. Jake explores one or two of the recommended websites and makes some notes about questions and comments he has on the topic in preparation for a class discussion the next day.

Jake's mother, Paula, owns a small bakery that specializes in weddings. Her days are hectic, and she finds herself working on her business wherever she happens to be. She keeps up with the day-to-day operation of her business while thinking of ways to improve and expand.

This week, she begins her workday in her home office. She checks her email and finds a message from a marketing firm she has contracted with requesting ideas for an upcoming ad campaign. She accesses a collaborative online document and adds some comments and suggestions.

She arrives at her business at 9:00 a.m. for a scheduled meeting with her staff to brainstorm some ideas for new recipes, products, and improved customer service. The kitchen has a large table that can accommodate all the staff, and she sets up chart paper to record everybody's thoughts. She takes a photo of their notes and posts them online so that everyone can have a chance to revisit them before their next meeting.

In her work office, Paula interviews an applicant via Skype for the part-time accountant's position that she advertised on Craigslist. After the interview, she goes to a local coffee shop for lunch, taking her tablet computer with her to surf the internet. She looks for the latest wedding trends and takes notes on her digital notepad for any ideas she wants to investigate further.

Paula's afternoon is a mixture of time at her desk working on schedules and planning, meeting with clients and vendors, and socializing with her staff. She likes to keep the work environment friendly and comfortable. She believes that promoting a family-like environment contributes to staff satisfaction and productivity.

At home, Paula relaxes with a glass of wine and reads a novel before getting dinner ready. While the chicken bakes, she looks through a print publication on entrepreneurship for ideas that she could use to improve her business.

Past, Present, and Future Learning

Paula's work requires flexible lifestyle, one that allows her to use technology effectively, collaborate with others, and adapt to the demands of any given moment or task. Jake's school environment is preparing him for the workplace of today, the type of environment his mother works in. But it is also preparing him for the workplace of tomorrow.

With the rapid pace of change, educators can't predict what jobs students like Jake might do in even 10 years, much less in 20. What we do know, however, is that today's students will probably not spend their whole workday within the walls of an office or factory. And whatever job they do, and however often they change careers, they will always need the digital-age skills, such as creativity, communication, and collaboration that they began to develop during their school days.

 **YOUR TURN**

Track how you spend your workday. Similar to the description of Paula's day, note any professional activities in which you engage. In particular, pay attention to when, where, and how you collaborate and communicate with others, work independently, and use technology.

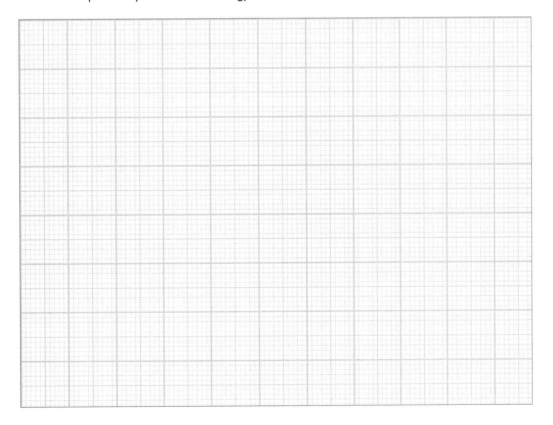

How are schools in your community preparing students for the demands of the modern workplace? Similar to the ways Jake is learning, what are some additional ways schools might better equip students for working in the digital age?

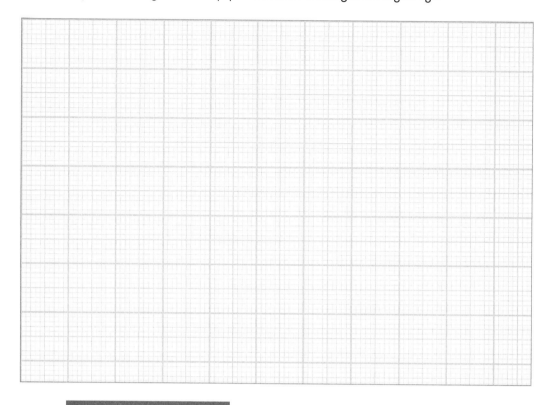

Schools of the Preindustrial Era

In ancient times, ordinary people participated in everyday tasks. This is how they learned the customs and values of the culture as well as the skills for working or managing a home. Learning experiences consisted of listening to stories and didactic talks, and observing the activities of experts who were usually members of an extended family. As children grew, their tasks gradually increased in difficulty until they were considered ready to proceed on their own. Formal education in abstract subjects such as mathematics and rhetoric, which were reserved for elite classes, was designed around the transmission of knowledge and cultural norms in generally passive environments where a leader passed on information that students learned, often by recitation and repetition.

Throughout the preindustrial era, no special school building was required for peasants and tradesmen to learn their crafts. The exception was for religious education that took place in a traditional, passive learning environment through sermons, exhortations, and study. The learning environment for most children of the preindustrial era was the world they lived in. And for most of the population of the earth, this level of education was sufficient to prepare them for the lives they would lead. Their options were quite limited, however, particularly if they happened to be female.

The Ford Model of Education

The advent of the industrial age in the 19th century created a necessity for a large number of educated workers who not only had basic reading, writing, and arithmetic skills but who also could easily conform to the requirements of large factories. The answer to these requirements was what Nair and his colleagues (2013) call the Ford model, or the cells-and-bells approach to education. Imagine a big, factory-like building. Inside is a hallway lined with individual classrooms. Inside each classroom are rows of desks facing the front of the room. Imagine a workday managed by a bell system that controls the beginning and ending of discrete class periods. This approach is based on four assumptions:

- All students are ready to learn the same thing at the same time in the same way from the same person.
- Learning is passive.
- One teacher can be all things (mentor, guide, lecturer, subject matter expert, caregiver) to 20–30 students simultaneously.
- Learning happens under teacher control (Nair et al., 2013).

There is much we could say about this model of schooling, but it hardly needs saying. Except for some early childhood learning environments, this model calls up a school design we all recognize, one that is still very much in use around the world, even in developed countries such as the United States. Sadly, this setting bears little resemblance to the workplace of today, much less the workplace of tomorrow.

Preparing Students for the Future Workplace

It's a long way from the apprenticeship model of learning in preindustrial times to the factory approach of the 19th century to the knowledge-based economy of the digital age. Work and life are very different now: more complex, more connected, and certainly more fast-paced. Unlike Jake, for most of today's students the gap between their out-of-school behavior and their school activities is considerable, both in the skills they are learning and the context in which they are learning them. This book aims to give educators the information and tools they need to begin to close the gap by looking at the ways that redesigned learning spaces can transform schools to better prepare students for the digital age.

Although not the only purpose of education, preparation for the workplace is certainly a critical goal of today's schools. Leaders in business and industry have been clear about the kinds of skills that will be needed in digital-age careers. Helping students develop these skills is a challenge that is made all the more difficult because many future careers don't yet exist! Whereas in the past, children could learn the skills of a career in school and expect to use those skills throughout their lives, tomorrow's workers must prepare to use technology, develop ideas, and solve problems in ways that can hardly even be imagined today.

Mohammed Khan of the World Bank lists some of the skills that students will need in the future workplace: "analytical thinking, problem-identification and solving, time management, adaptability, and the capacity for collaboration and effective communication" (Kahn, 2014). According to Amber Golden Raskin, the executive director of business development and operations at SCVi, a charter school in Castaic, California, teaching these skills requires classroom spaces where, "students can collaborate and participate in real-life environments where they can learn how to work on teams; that's what they'll be doing in the work world" (McCrea, *THE Journal*, 2012).

A 2013 Gallup poll conducted with the support of Microsoft Partners in Learning and the Pearson Foundation asked workers about the connections among their secondary and post-secondary instruction, their aspirations as students, and the quality of their work lives. The survey found that people who were taught digital-age skills in their schooling had greater aspirations for learning. The effectiveness of this learning depended, of course, on the quality of the instruction. The survey found that students must have frequent and broad practice with these digital-age skills, such as activities in the context of real-life problem solving, if this learning is to have an impact on their work life.

The findings of this survey pose a challenge for today's educators who want to prepare students for the digital age: half of the respondents replied that they had developed most of the skills they use on the job *outside of school*. Additionally, while 86% of those responding said they did use computers and technology for school projects, only 14% of them used technology to collaborate, one of the most critical skills for the digital-age workplace. Clearly, there is work to be done in today's classrooms if we want students to be successful not only in their future careers but in their social, political, and personal lives.

Digital-Age Learners and Technology

There's no question that today's students depend on technology far more than their predecessors. For these "digital natives," as they are often called, the lines separating technology for learning and technology for fun are blurred, as are the lines that separate learning inside and outside of the classroom.

A survey conducted by Harris Poll for Pearson (2014) found that 80% of all students surveyed said they had used a laptop to do schoolwork during the past year. Students are also increasingly leveraging mobile devices for learning. The percentage of elementary students using tablets rose from 52% to 66% in just one year from 2013 to 2014. Although, at 43%, high school students are most likely to use their mobile phones for class work, middle school and elementary students reported following the trend: 20% and 17% respectively.

Interestingly, this behavior occurs in school environments where the use of mobile phones is often banned in the classroom. Not surprisingly, according to the survey, over half of all students at any grade level would like to use their mobile devices in school more often than they currently do.

You could say that today's young people are the most 24-7-connected generation in history. With their smartphones always within reach, digital-age learners have come to rely on technology to communicate and collaborate. A 2014 survey of teen-agers found, not surprisingly, that students are heavy users of social media and microblogging platforms such as Facebook, Instagram, and Twitter. However, by far, the most popular method of communication through technology is text messaging, where the average number of text messages exchanged by teens each day is 30 (Lenhart & Page, 2015).

Of course, it's impossible to keep completely current with the technology that teens use the most. It seems that the more popular a particular tool becomes in the mainstream, the less young people want to use it. Still, the trend of constant connection is not likely to diminish over time, and educators must find ways to incorporate this type of virtual collaboration and communication into the learning process. It is what digital-age students want, and it will happen with or without the beneficial guidance of educators.

ISTE Standards

Jake seamlessly integrates technology into all aspects of his life and demonstrates the true impact technology can have on the way we learn, work, and play. Consider how closely the following ISTE Standards for Students (ISTE Standards•S) align with the daily activities in the lives of a digital-age learner such as Jake:

1. Creativity and innovation—Students demonstrate creative thinking, construct knowledge, and develop innovative products and processes using technology.
2. Communication and collaboration—Students use digital media and environments to communicate and work collaboratively, including at a distance, to support individual learning and contribute to the learning of others.
3. Research and information fluency—Students apply digital tools to gather, evaluate, and use information.
4. Critical thinking, problem solving, and decision making—Students use critical thinking skills to plan and conduct research, manage projects, solve problems, and make informed decisions using appropriate digital tools and resources.
5. Digital citizenship—Students understand human, cultural, and societal issues related to technology and practice legal and ethical behavior.
6. Technology operations and concepts—Students demonstrate a sound understanding of technology concepts, systems, and operations (ISTE, 2007).

Visit the ISTE website at iste.org/standards for additional resources and information about the ISTE Standards•S.

Designing Learning Spaces for Digital-Age Students

What does the proliferation of accessible technology mean for educators who want to design learning spaces for digital-age students? First, it means educators must acknowledge that students not only benefit from having this technology at their fingertips but that they expect to have it available whenever and wherever they need it. Second, they must believe that when technology is integrated into meaningful, real-life learning experiences, students will be engaged and motivated to learn. Third, they must accept that in the digital age, ubiquitous technology access is a given, and so it must be a significant feature of any digital-age learning space.

Another significant consequence of the technology habits of today's students and tomorrow's workers is the expectation that learning can happen anywhere and anytime. Like Jake and Paula, digital-age students and workers do not limit their work areas to the four walls of the school or the office. They move from large-group spaces to semi-private nooks, from inside to outside, and from quiet, sheltered places to noisy, chaotic public places.

Neither are these individuals limited to learning materials recommended by teachers and other authorities. Technology enables learners of all ages to personalize their own learning, look for the resources they need, and design their own learning paths. Mobile technology expands the learning environment both figuratively and literally. And today's schools must support this critical aspect of digital-age life.

YOUR TURN

Interview students about how they use technology in and out of school. Consider using some of the following questions:

- What types of devices do they frequently use or own?
- How do they use technology for personal tasks?
- How do they use technology for school-related tasks?
- Does their technology use in school align with their expectations and/or needs?

After gathering student responses, consider implications for ideal learning spaces. How can learning spaces be designed to better accommodate the ways in which students currently use technology and want to use technology?

Learning Spaces for Digital-Age Learners

Paula, our small business owner, does not work in the restricted environment of the assembly line, the iconic workplace image of the 20th century. Likewise, our student Jake does not attend a classic cells-and-bells school. Instead, both use a range of technologies and physical spaces to work on personal, professional, and academic tasks.

P21 (formerly Partnership for 21st Century Skills) describes the kind of learning spaces needed to meet the needs of digital-age students and teachers. This learning environment:

- Supports professional learning communities that enable educators to collaborate, share best practices, and integrate 21st century skills into classroom practice.
- Enables students to learn in relevant, real world 21st century contexts…
- Provides 21st century architectural and interior designs for group, team, and individual learning.
- Supports expanded community and international involvement in learning, both face-to-face and online (P21, n.d.).

Although all educators aspire to prepare students for success, few schools are designed to take advantage of what we know about learning spaces. Combined with effective pedagogy and qualified teachers, we can transform schools into responsive, flexible environments that engage students and help them develop the skills and knowledge they need for the future.

 **YOUR TURN**

Create a Venn diagram similar the figure below and use it to compare and contrast the form and function of learning spaces in the industrial era and ideal learning spaces of the digital age.

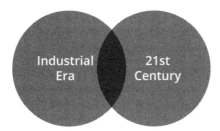

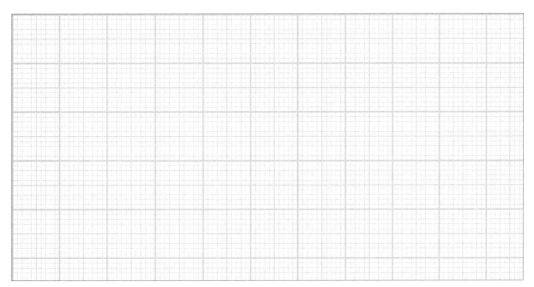

 REFLECT & DISCUSS

1. Jake's experience in school aligns with the realities of his life. How does this compare to the experience of students in your community?
2. What skills do you think are most imperative for your students to develop for working and living in the future?
3. How does the instructional pedagogy employed in your classroom, school, or district align with the current learning spaces?
4. Given the current status of learning spaces in your community, what are the biggest challenges for administrators and teachers attempting to incorporate digital-age skills?

 **CASE STUDY**

It's All in the Blend

Metro Nashville Public Schools Learns That with Big Grants Come Big Responsibilities

Metropolitan Nashville Public Schools (MNPS) has a lot of things going for it: strong district leadership, dedicated funding, and a supportive state partner. And it isn't lacking in vision, either: in September 2013, the MNPS Board of Education approved a strategic plan with the goal of making Metropolitan Nashville Public Schools the highest-performing urban school district in the United States by 2018.

As the 42nd-largest urban school district in the country, encompassing an area of about 525 square miles, serving roughly 85,000 students speaking more than 70 different languages, you would think progressive institutional change would come slowly.

Think again.

Metro Nashville Demographics (as of 2014)

- 86,000 students
- 5,786 teachers
- 4,227 staff
- 157 schools (73 elementary schools, 33 middle schools, 25 high schools, 18 charter schools, and eight specialty schools)
- 72.4% free- and reduced-lunch eligible
- 14.3% limited English proficient
- 19% Hispanic; 32% Caucasian; 45% African American; 4% Asian
- Urban location encompassing the city of Nashville and the surrounding county

Space Is the Place for Learning

Through a competitive grant process, the Metropolitan Nashville Public Schools district allocated 1 million dollars of RTT (Race to the Top) money to their schools through a competitive grant process in order to fund sweeping renovations to its facilities. The aim was to incorporate technology and establish model learning spaces throughout the district. Hume Fogg Magnet High School (the oldest high school in the district, dating from 1912) had a vast, underutilized space that connected two wings of the school. The district turned this area into a collaborative learning space that could be used by students throughout the school. The room has six TVs on rolling stands and tables and chairs that roll to accommodate multiple learning scenarios. By design, the environment can be configured in countless ways.

Figure 1.1: Nashville's completely renovated Hillwood High School Library featuring flexible spaces for research and collaboration

Another high school in the district, McGavock High School, had locker bay areas about the size of a small classroom. These locker bays were unused by students, so they were converted into internet cafés. One of the new internet cafés, similar to a coffee shop atmosphere but without food, has six cubicles that students can use to do online work for their classes or do credit recovery online. Three collaborative areas feature high-top tables with stools, comfortable chairs, and mounted TVs.

The middle schools in the district added new tables in their classrooms instead of individual desks. They also created spaces with computers, large-screen TVs for collaborative technology use, and comfortable seating. The walls were painted with whiteboard paint and a large interactive wall was installed, which allows 15 students to approach a wall and write, draw, or doodle at the same time. The whiteboard walls also have interactive projectors, making the wall an interactive whiteboard.

"When you walk into a restaurant, you scope out the room and look for a comfortable and clean space. If you see dirt and disarray, then you go somewhere else," says Kecia Ray, executive director of Learning Technology and Library Services for Metropolitan Nashville Public Schools. "That's the same impact learning spaces have on engaging students. When students walk into inviting, interactive, and comfortable classrooms, they are much more likely to be engaged and interactive within their learning experience. Classrooms that are cluttered or focused on adults rather than students are not places where students want to learn…just ask them!"

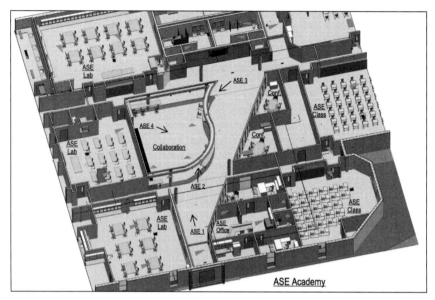

Figure 1.2: Concept designs for Stratford Stem Magnet High School's Academy of Science and Engineering

Pumping up the Technology

The district's active learning spaces are amplified with technology to support both personalized and blended learning approaches. Buena Vista Elementary Enhanced Option school, for example, features adjustable tables and chairs in every classroom, including a teacher desk that can recharge 10 tablet devices at a time. Each classroom has carpet to accommodate reading groups and comfortable multipurpose seating for performing activities such as reading books or using devices. The school has blended instruction in grades K–4, and student classes have blocks for blended ELA (English language arts) as well as blended math, with a computer for every student in every classroom.

According to Dr. Ray, these ambitious changes in classroom spaces and instructional design have resulted in substantial rewards (8 to 10-point increases in ELA and Math scores from 2013 state standardized test scores to 2014 scores).

"Buena Vista is comprised of 95% FARL (free and reduced-price lunch), 70% transient, and 30% homeless students," Dr. Ray clarifies. "So it was important to the principal and myself to ensure that this school had the best of the best. And this emphasis on creating a thriving environment for the students while they were in school has paid off in dividends. In every school where we've implemented blended learning, we are seeing at minimum eight-point gains in academic achievement from 2013 state standardized test scores to 2014 scores. If there is such a thing as a silver bullet, I believe blended learning is the closest we've come to date."

Metropolitan Nashville Public Schools is one of the most diverse school districts in the country, which is one reason why the district's strategic plan focuses on personalized and blended learning for all students. Typical classrooms may have carts loaded with laptops or tablet devices to accommodate students who don't bring their own devices to school. The focus is on building and providing a learning environment that any device could connect to, from anywhere, at any time. This platform ensures that no matter what devices are purchased, loaned, or brought from home, students can have seamless and dependable access to content and instruction.

Building a Foundation for Blended Learning

And the same approach that went into providing a robust and flexible technological platform to support blended learning initiatives also went into the design of the physical spaces in which that learning happens. Some of the district's libraries, for example, feature internet cafés (some even serve food or welcome students in for lunch), cozy reading nooks, self-checkout stations, and collaborative spaces.

Bringing this level of change to a district of this size takes strong leadership. To facilitate innovations in space design and technology infrastructure, the principals of Metropolitan Nashville Public Schools are given budget flexibility to support school-based decisions within the constraint of the district's strategic plan and their own local school improvement plans. Principals were involved in the development of the district's action plan to better align with their own school improvement plans, and are given support from the central office to implement these school plans.

"You've got to engage a lot of people in the design process to make sure you get it right while not being afraid to do something different," Dr. Ray explains. "Learning spaces include furniture, lighting, flooring, interactive technology, wireless access points, and engaging—oftentimes adaptive—software, so you've got to be sure to consider *all* of it!"

Dr. Ray, who oversees the Learning Technology and Library Services department, is in charge of instructional and learning technologies in each of the district's 6,000 classrooms as well as the collections in their 132 libraries. Designing learning spaces is a key component of this role as well. Learning technologies include all instructional software: everything from digital textbooks and RTI (Response to Intervention) to games and physical education software, as well as the hardware to support interactive instruction.

Figure 1.3: The open and accommodating layout of the Apollo Middle School Library

Process Makes Perfect

The Learning Technology and Library Services department helped schools to implement technology integration and blended learning within their buildings. They worked to ensure that all of the district's school libraries have high-quality collections and engaging learning environments, and that each school identifies a tech lead to support the overall plan for technology within the school's improvement plan. The department also has a team of people who work with schools on design and build phases. The library services team works with architects on the design of the spaces and then with interior designers to make the selections on everything from fabric and furniture to fixtures and floor coverings. They sign off on final installations before occupancy and then work with the schools on the "punch list" to correct flaws. They are also involved in the network infrastructure needs for the facility from beginning to end, and they collaboratively determine such details as where boxes should be located for cable and power as well as the location and logistics of Wi-Fi and interactive boards. Because the school librarians play such a significant role in the planning of spaces, they are able to support teachers and students in utilizing those spaces.

Based on a solid foundation of innovation, creativity, and integrity, Metropolitan Nashville Public Schools has taken public education fearlessly into the digital age. The MNPS Learning Technology and Library Services department is providing learning opportunities to those who meet students on the front line and make the largest impact on students—the teachers. These opportunities are also moving into the digital age via innovative multiple delivery platforms, such as virtual, asynchronous classrooms, real-time webinars, and traditional face-to-face instruction. And this innovation is evident in the district's learning spaces, where classrooms, libraries, and collaboration spaces are alive with engagement and dynamism.

"When you go to banks, restaurants, shopping centers or even office parks, do you see the same work environment you saw twenty years ago? *No!*" Dr. Ray says. "So, why shouldn't schools similarly morph into environments that will be more engaging and interesting to our students? When I walk into a classroom I want to see students buzzing about from one space to another with little need to ask direction of the teacher. I also want to see appropriate technology being used by students for learning. Whether it's nice furnishings, high-quality technology, or the best software money can buy, our students deserve the very best we have to offer."

CHAPTER 2

Teaching and Learning in the Digital Age

Nobody knows exactly what the future will bring. Fifty years ago, who would have believed we would be carrying powerful computers in our pockets but *not* riding around in flying cars? Still, we have some pretty good ideas about what the future will require of today's students. And even if we can't always predict the successful technologies of the future, we can be certain that teachers will be greatly challenged when preparing students to succeed in our constantly changing cultural, social, and technological environment.

Recognizing the shortcomings of knowledge transmission and rote memory exercises as teaching methods is hardly a digital-age innovation. Beyond the apprenticeship and family and community enculturation models from the earliest of human history—you can't get much more active than that—for at least two centuries educators have proposed school environments that help students actively grapple with real-life problems.

Research has decidedly refuted the traditional teacher-centered approach to learning. A review of the literature on teaching for deep learning found that "Traditional academic approaches—narrow tasks that emphasize memorization or the application of simple algorithms—won't develop students who are critical thinkers or students who can write and speak effectively" (Barron & Darling-Hammond, 2008), skills that are critical for success in the digital age.

Learning Spaces for Digital-Age Learning Models

A desire to provide students with learning experiences that deepen their content knowledge and prepare them for the future has long been a concern for educational theorists and practitioners. Over time, a few pedagogical models have emerged that incorporate what we know about how students learn. Taking a look at these models can help us think about how the spaces in which students learn can be designed to promote and enhance this kind of meaningful learning.

Active Learning

The term *active learning* has been prominent in educational circles for decades. Considered in this book as the intersection of technology, pedagogy, and space, active learning refers to a wide range of approaches that place students at the center of the learning process.

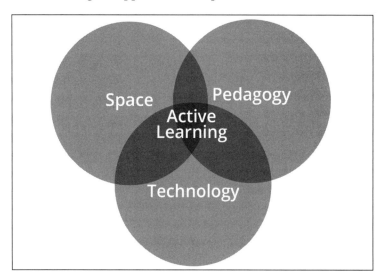

Figure 2.1: Venn diagram showing Active Learning as the intersection of Technology, Space, and Pedagogy.

The term is often used in contrast to *passive learning*, an approach that depicts students as the receptacles for knowledge transmitted by teachers and textbooks. Traditional class-room design, while ideal for an environment where students merely absorb information from outside sources, is inadequate for supporting students as they construct their own knowledge. Table 2.1 compares the two approaches applied to middle school math lessons on probability:

Table 2.1: Comparison of Passive and Active Learning

Instructional Approach	Lesson: Probability, Middle School Math	Learning Space
Passive learning	1. The teacher introduces the topic of probability and presents the basic concepts in a whole-class demonstration and lecture format. 2. Students individually complete a few probability exercises in class and complete the remaining problems as homework. 3. The next day, students trade papers to correct each other's work while the teacher "goes over" the answers. 4. The teacher presents the next topic in the sequence and assigns practice exercises.	A classroom with individual desks all with a view of the teacher's presentation. Individual spaces for students to work on assignments by themselves.

Instructional Approach	Lesson: Probability, Middle School Math	Learning Space
Active learning	1. The teacher puts students in pairs to play "Rock, Paper, Scissors" 15 times to think about probability. 2. Students record the results of their games in an online document. 3. Student pairs join into small groups to discuss the results and answer open-ended questions about experimental and theoretical probability. 4. Each group shares its conclusions with the whole class. 5. The teacher conducts a whole-class discussion on their conclusions. 6. Students write in their journals about what they thought about probability before and after the experiment. 7. The teacher engages students in a whole-class discussion where they formalize learning from the experiment.	Places for students to meet as pairs while being observed by teacher. Small-group spaces under teacher supervision with access to technology. Large-group area with view of screen for presentations. Large-group area with view of each other for discussions. Individual spaces under teacher observation where students can complete individual work quietly.

If you ask teachers who approach instruction from a traditional, passive learning perspective to describe the activities in their classroom, you are likely to get responses like:

- "I'm covering Chapter 11 today."
- "Students are working on a study guide for a unit test."
- "I'm showing a video on the Battle of Gettysburg."
- "I'm reviewing the symbolism in *Huckleberry Finn*."
- "We're checking last night's homework and then moving on to parallelograms."

By contrast, teachers with an active learning perspective will describe different kinds of activities that are often facilitated, rather than directed by, the teacher.

- "Students are watching a video on plate tectonics, taking notes, and then working with a group to create a graphic organizer of the most important information."
- "Students are working with a partner to interpret a poem and share their ideas with the class."
- "In small groups, students are brainstorming ideas for a statistics project."
- "I'm doing a mini-lesson on how to use the project rubric to give each other feedback. Then students are sharing their presentations on World War I for peer review."

Nearly all teachers today incorporate some aspect of active learning into their instruction. They do so because many student-centered activities, such as think-pair-share activities, small group discussions, and personal responses can be successfully integrated into a mostly traditional classroom environment. That being said, a flexible learning space can make it easier for teachers to expand their repertoire of instructional strategies to include more student-centered options.

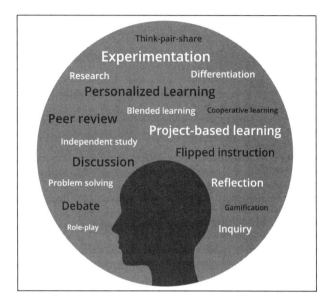

Figure 2.2: Teaching and learning models

YOUR TURN

Use the following checklist to assess your readiness for active learning. Check a box indicating the level of your agreement with each statement. Please note that the activity is not meant to judge your teaching; instead its goal is to encourage reflection about instructional styles that are conducive to active learning spaces and digital-age learning.

Agree	Somewhat Agree	Disagree	Statement
❑	❑	❑	I am comfortable giving students control over what and how they learn.
❑	❑	❑	I expect students to reflect and monitor their learning progress.
❑	❑	❑	I hold students accountable for committing to their education.

Agree	Somewhat Agree	Disagree	Statement
❑	❑	❑	I focus on explicitly teaching skills not just the content.
❑	❑	❑	I strive to create life-long learners.
❑	❑	❑	I provide and promote opportunities for collaboration.
❑	❑	❑	I want students to responsibly leverage technology and other resources to augment the learning process.
❑	❑	❑	I give students choices about how they present their learning.
❑	❑	❑	I believe that learning gets messy and that different perspectives should be celebrated.
❑	❑	❑	I am comfortable with a noisy classroom as long as students are engaged and actively learning.

From what you have learned, sketch two contrasting spaces in the space below: one that is ideal for active learning and one that is ideal for passive learning.

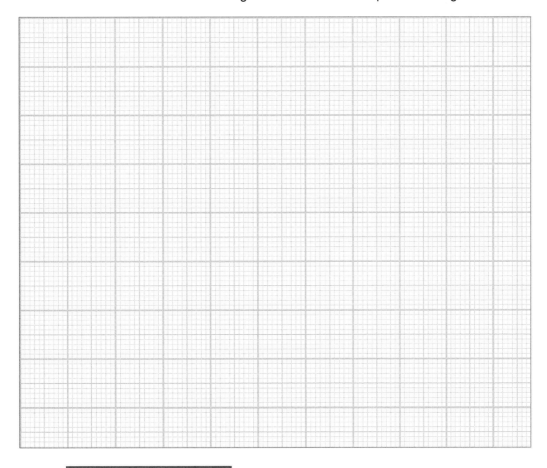

Types of Active Learning Spaces

Learning could—and *should*—happen anywhere. A learning space can be any place where a student is actively engaged with new concepts and ideas. Table 2.2 below shows ways of looking at the kinds of spaces that support active learning.

Table 2.2: Types of Active Learning Spaces

Space	Description	Examples	Active Learning Experiences
Private/Alone	Private areas without visual or audio distraction	Study carrels, private rooms, blocked out classroom spaces, outdoor seating	Reading, writing, reflecting, research
Public/Alone	Individual study spaces with social connections, often a matter of personal preference	Classroom desks, café seating, libraries, park-like seating	Research, reading, writing, individual work on collaborative projects
Private/Together	Spaces with accommodations for a range of group sizes and learning modes	Large tables, grouped seating in public areas like libraries and cafeterias, groups of chairs with whiteboards, dyads and triads, outside benches, playgrounds	Small group discussions, brainstorming, collaborative project work, partner sharing, getting and giving feedback, socializing, informal play
Public/Together	Places to support sharing of information or performances with large groups of individuals	Whole classroom arrangement, auditoriums, athletic fields, community meeting places	Teacher and student presentations, guest speakers, large-group discussions and sharing, performances, organized athletics

(Steelcase Education, 2013)

David Thornburg, in his book *From the Campfire to the Holodeck* (2014), uses time-honored concepts to describe the kinds of learning spaces in digital-age schools:

- Campfires: Places where a large group gathers to share the same experience through listening and/or watching a performance or presentation.
- Watering holes: Spaces for small group collaboration and socializing.
- Caves: Individual spaces with barriers to audio and visual stimuli for quiet reflection.
- Life: Real world spaces where students apply what they are learning to authentic situations and problems.

Regardless of the metaphors you prefer to use to describe learning spaces, the actual environment must provide students and teachers with the flexibility they need to access the right kind of space at the right time.

Blended and Flipped Learning

The flipped and blended learning instructional models incorporate technology to create a more student-centered environment. A blended approach uses both face-to-face interactions and digital resources to give students the most meaningful experiences possible.

> Blended learning is any time a student learns at least in part at a supervised brick-and-mortar location away from home and at least in part through online delivery with some element of student control over time, place, path, and/or pace (Horn & Staker, 2011).

The blended learning model has become for many classrooms today the usual way to design teaching and learning. Virtual experiences in such classrooms are seamlessly integrated with activities throughout the learning process. This approach increases the likelihood that students in a classroom will be engaged in a variety of technology-centric activities that require different kinds of learning spaces, many of which need access to technology.

A specific type of blended classroom is the flipped classroom. The term *flipping* means that the traditional order and location of learning activities is reversed. In a flipped learning environment, students access content information outside of the classroom and apply that information in the classroom. For example, to prepare for a face-to-face class session students would, on their own outside of class, read a passage or watch a video online that the teacher produced. Students, working at their own pace, take notes and consider questions in any location where they have internet access. Later, in the classroom, students then interact with peers in a student-centered activity where they apply what they have learned through problems, projects, or other authentic learning experiences. These are tasks that would be given as homework in traditional learning environments. When learning is flipped, during the application stage (the challenging part of the learning process), students get support from their peers. In addition, the teacher is available for one-to-one or small group explanations.

Voices from a Flipped Classroom

Stacey Roshan, a teacher at Bullis School in Maryland, flipped her AP calculus class and collected the following comments from her students about the experience.

"The format of this class allows us to work at our own pace. If we need to pause a video and rewind, it is much simpler than interrupting a teacher during class and asking her to repeat what she said. I also love that we have class time to work with other students and ask individual questions. Another great aspect of this format is that it reduces stress because it is so easy to make up the work at home by watching the videos."

"I can get help with whatever problems I need instead of struggling with hard problems at home with no help."

"The video lectures allow for a student to work at their own pace. And it is important to note that all students have different strengths. For instance, I watched some videos three times, and skimmed through other ones" (2012).

The fact that flipped classrooms allow students to collaborate with peers and teachers in meaningful learning experiences during class time normally reserved for routine instruction makes it an appealing learning model. Flipped instruction can be done in a traditional classroom. However, a digital-age active learning environment can better accommodate the kinds of activities that that students would do at home and in the classroom, thereby meeting the needs of all students.

Distance Learning

Digital age distance learning is a method of learning where subject-based lectures or presentations are broadcast over the internet, allowing students to take part in classes wherever they are. Distance learning classrooms require specific technology and design requirements to best facilitate this unique form of learning.

For capturing lectures and presentations, high-definition video cameras are essential, while well-placed LCD displays are ideal for viewing. Some distance learning classrooms feature videoconferencing and webcasting capabilities for more interactive discussions and functionality.

Lectures can be displayed from a PC or laptop onto LCD screens for improved visibility. This allows students to easily follow a distance learning lecture as well as the simultaneous back-and-forth interaction of an in-class educator or facilitator. The infrastructure, the lighting, and the acoustics should all be carefully considered when designing a room for distance learning. For example, acoustic panels can be used to eliminate distracting noise, and dimmable lights help maintain optimal viewing conditions. Small details such as these can make a huge impact on the learning experience.

Project-Based Learning

At the far end of the active learning spectrum is project-based learning. In today's educational jargon, you will hear the terms *project-based* or *problem-based* learning. Although enthusiasts of these methods can provide definitions and examples that differentiate them, for our purposes they both aim to accomplish the same goal: to engage students in learning through the application of content knowledge and skills to real-life situations.

Calling an activity a *project* doesn't necessarily make it an authentic, meaningful experience for students. Many so-called projects connect superficially to content standards and require little in the way of deep thinking. John Larmer and John R. Mergendoller of the Buck Institute of Education, an organization whose mission is to help teachers implement project-based learning successfully, list eight characteristics of high quality projects.

- *A need to know.* The project is introduced to students in a way that engages their thinking and curiosity, and prompts questions that must be answered through investigation and problem solving.
- *A driving question.* A good driving question captures the heart of the project in

clear, compelling language, which gives students a sense of purpose and challenge. The question should be provocative, open-ended, complex, and linked to the core of what you want students to learn.

- *Student voice and choice.* The more choice within a project, the better. Making choices encourages intrinsic motivation and helps students develop self-management skills.

- *Impactful content*: The learning in a well-designed project-based experience centers around knowledge and skills that are important, relevant, and tied to standards.

- *21st century skills.* Good, complex projects require a range of 21st century skills including collaboration, communication, and creativity. Most projects today, either by requirement or by student choice, also require technology skills such as information literacy and new media literacies.

- *Inquiry and innovation.* Projects become more meaningful when students conduct real inquiry, not research that consists of copying and pasting from online sources. A good project asks students to investigate primary sources, conduct experiments, and evaluate conflicting information.

- *Feedback and revision.* Giving and receiving substantive feedback is an important skill for the 21st century workplace in the information age. As students think critically about their own work and the work of their peers, they also begin to internalize the standards for high-quality work.

- *A publicly presented product.* Few students are motivated to do their best work when the only audience is their teacher. Projects provide students with not only the skills and content they need to be academically successful, public presentations help them practice the communication skills they need to successfully explain and defend their ideas (Buck Institute of Education, 2010).

Sample Project: A Case of the Cooties

Seventh grade students at a middle school that is part of the High Tech High network of schools in San Diego complete a project investigating the origin of different diseases, how they are spread, and how they can be prevented. To demonstrate their learning, students create either a game or a Flash animation.

The project is designed to meet five learning goals:

- A thorough understanding of a disease
- How the disease interacts with the human body
- The impact of the disease on humans around the world
- Time management
- Project management

Continued on next page

Continued from previous page

Brent Spimak, a multimedia instructor from High Tech High, reflects on one aspect of the project:

> I do not have much background in Adobe Flash, so it was challenging to troubleshoot the students' work because I was learning it along with them.... There were often times when we did not find an answer. This frustrated students at times, but I think they learned that their teacher is not the smartest one in the class. Other students stepped up and helped them out with their projects, and this is the most ideal learning environment during a long-term project (Projects at High Tech High, n.d.).

Components of an Active Learning Space

Authentic learning projects, like life projects, do not confine themselves to just one subject area: They are interdisciplinary. Reading and writing are parts of many projects, as are the arts through graphic design and multimedia production. The physical arrangement of a school should then support communication among subject areas as well as access to materials, technology, and experts in different domains.

Consider the following glimpses into student activities in an active learning environment:

ISTE Essential Condition: Student-Centered Learning

"Planning, teaching and assessment all center on the needs and abilities of the students" (ISTE, 2009).

Student-centered learning is a critical element in effective technology integrations. Beyond simply adding technology into classrooms, it is essential that a teaching and learning pedagogy leverages technology to deepen relevant, standards-based learning experiences. Active learning spaces that allow for varied student learning activities with and without technology can support a shift toward a student-centered educational approach.

- Students in a language arts class contact a local video producer through Skype to learn more about how to shoot and edit a video they are creating about a book their group has chosen to read.
- A math teacher notices from observational formative assessment that students working on a statistics project are drawing incorrect conclusions based on their misconceptions about probability. She draws the whole class together for some direct instruction and guided practice on the topic.
- After completing an interdisciplinary project, students take time to reflect on their learning and to set goals for future work.

- As an introduction to a Science, Technology, Engineering, Art, and Mathematics (STEAM) project, a teacher asks students to use their smartphones to take videos of examples of simple machines around the school grounds. When they return to the classroom, they use the videos to get ideas and then to document the creation of simple machines from everyday office supplies.

In an active learning environment, whether it is one that includes some student-centered activities, blended or flipped learning approaches, or full-blown project-based learning, learners need different kinds of spaces to meet their needs. The following list is just a sample of the kinds of spaces that support digital-age learning:

- Small-group areas for discussing, brainstorming, planning, and creating
- Large-group areas for whole-class instruction and presentations
- Technology-rich areas for activities such as online research, virtual communication, media production, and app development
- Quiet, solitary areas for individual reading, writing, and reflection
- Community accessible areas for sharing, parent meetings, and presentations
- Makerspaces where students have access to technology as well as hands-on materials

 **YOUR TURN**

Is your classroom ready for active learning? Consider the following activities common in active learning classrooms, and then assess a learning space with which you are familiar.

Activity	What works?	What doesn't work?
Small group collaboration		
Large group discussion and instruction		
Use of technology to gather, process, and synthesize learning		

Continued on next page

Continued from previous page

Independent study		
Presentation of learning to larger community		
Experimentation and hands-on learning		

Learning Spaces for Digital-Age Skills

One of the main drawbacks to a passive learning environment is that it provides few opportunities for students to develop the skills that are so important in the digital-age workplace. When teachers control the topics and pace of learning, the ways students access knowledge, and the ways they demonstrate what they've learned, students can't develop their creativity, collaboration, and problem-solving skills. And when the only audience for student work is the teacher, students can't develop the flexible, effective communication skills they need in a digital age.

Communication and Digital-Age Standards

Communication skills are addressed in digital-age academic standards, particularly as they relate to forming good arguments.

"Mathematically proficient students understand and use stated assumptions, definitions, and previously established results in constructing arguments. They make conjectures and build a logical progression of statements to explore the truth of their conjectures" (National Governors Association Center for Best Practices, 2010).

"Any education in science and engineering needs to develop students' ability to read and produce domain-specific text. As such, every science or engineering lesson is in part a language lesson, particularly reading and producing the genres of texts that are intrinsic to science and engineering" (Quinn et al., 2012).

Collaboration Skills

All digital-age skills are, of course, important. But it is collaboration that is often identified as among the most critical skills for the future workplace. It is also fundamental to active learning. Collaboration in the classroom can meet two important instructional goals. First, the development of collaboration skills is itself an important learning objective. And second, research conclusively shows that well-designed collaborative activities contribute to improved academic achievement (Lai, 2011).

Incorporating collaboration into a traditional classroom environment poses many challenges. Students need spaces where they can meet with each other. They need access to the tools that support the kinds of thinking that helps them learn, often at the same time that other students are working alone or with the teacher. Digital-age learning environments also need to support collaboration among adults, mentors, and peers outside of the classroom, often facilitated by technology. Thinking carefully about how a learning space can support the kind of collaboration that builds confident learners is an important step in designing effective learning environments.

Communication Skills

In the industrial learning environment of the 20th century, communication skills such as writing and speaking were relegated to the language arts class; but in digital-age learning environments, communication is a critical component of every subject area.

Communication in digital-age learning environments takes on far more forms than it does in traditional classrooms. Gone are the days when an occasional essay or speech in an English class meets learning objectives. Today, throughout the curriculum, students are expected to explain their thinking, persuade others of their opinions, and engage readers and listeners. And students must do so not only with words but also with graphic and multimedia elements.

Creativity Skills

Creativity is another critical skill in the digital age. We all recognize creativity when we see it—in the gadgets we use every day, in the art that makes us appreciate and think about the world around us, and in the ideas that challenge us and help us grow. P21 identifies creativity as one of the most prized skills for the future, and yet the traditional classroom environment often presents more of a challenge than a support for creative thinking.

Digital-Age Skills in the Classroom

Consider how the following project in a high school language arts class addresses the digital-age skills of collaboration, communication, and creativity; and how the design of the learning space supports learning.

Small groups of students choose an allegorical novel to read together from a list provided by their teacher. After they have finished reading their books, each group is asked to create a 3-dimensional object that illustrates their interpretation of the allegory presented in the book, including a quote from the book for each component of their object.

Each group, supplied with chart paper, meets in a small-group space to brainstorm ideas for their project. One group decides to make a mobile illustrating their interpretation of *Lord of the Flies*. With a general idea of what they want to create, the group works at a large-screen computer to design and create their mobile. Two students, both are taking a STEAM course, volunteer to use a 3D printer to create some pieces for their mobile. Other group members get art materials, including glue and paint, from a convenient storage location. They put all the pieces of their project together in a production space that features large tables.

The activity concludes with an oral presentation of their mobile to other small groups in a small presentation space. The different groups take turns describing their projects and analyses of their chosen novels.

Creativity flourishes in an environment where students can take risks and fail, where they have options about what they learn, how they learn, and how to demonstrate what they have learned. Although you can certainly find examples of student creativity in the most traditional of classrooms, flexible learning spaces supported by effective instruction can bring out creativity in all students.

Creative thinking is both collaborative and solitary. Students can be inspired to create surprising and useful projects by interacting with peers and mentors. They can get feedback from others and use examples of admired work as models for their own creations. The creative process, however, also requires that individuals find time and space for reflection and self-assessment, for thinking through ideas, and for imagining how an idea might be brought to fruition.

Creativity is both chaotic and orderly. At the "anything goes" stage, the free flow of ideas is crucial. Students need spaces that support interaction and allow them to keep a record of their thoughts, whether it is digitally, on whiteboards, or chart paper. At some point, however, the ideas must be made real, and a clear process must be followed to transform an idea into a reality. Spaces for the development of a creative idea might include tools and resources such as powerful computers with specialized software, 3D printers, art supplies, or building materials.

Technology Integration

Today's students already use technology, particularly mobile devices, for educational purposes. Increasingly they expect to be allowed, if not encouraged, to use them within the school walls. (In later chapters, we describe concrete ways to design spaces that provide students with the technology they need, when they need it.)

It's no surprise that students want to use technology. But is it good for them? Does it actually engage them in deep and meaningful learning? Does it help them meet content standards and learn digital-age skills? The answer is—it depends.

Mostly, the success of technology integration depends on what students are doing with technology. Simply integrating technology alongside traditional teaching practices may not have a positive impact on student learning. For example, an analysis of data from the National Assessment of Educational Progress (NAEP) found a negative relationship between students' math scores and the frequency of their technology use if the technology was used simply for drill and practice, similar to paper worksheets used in the traditional classroom (Warschauer & Matchuchniak, 2010).

There is considerable evidence, however, that technology can contribute to deep learning of content as well as the development of important digital-age skills. Using technology for learning activities such as simulations and writing show a positive effect on learning

(Warschauer & Matuchniak, 2010). Perhaps the most important way to use technology in a digital-age learning environment is by engaging students in the creation of content through project-based learning. These kinds of activities, combined with teacher support and collaboration with peers and others, result in "stronger engagement, self-efficacy, attitudes toward school, and skill development" (Darling-Hammond, Zielezinski & Goldman, 2014).

Research shows that the use of technology can motivate students, especially those who are disengaged from the learning process. In a 2010 report by Project Tomorrow, teachers reported that technology improved students' "cognitive, affective, behavioral, academic, and social engagement." They also said that it increased skills and dispositions such as "taking initiative and responsibility for learning, using resources wisely, time on task, and having interest and desire to pursue information and learn in and beyond classrooms" (Taylor & Parsons, 2011).

Designers of digital-age learning spaces are challenged to provide students with the necessary access to technologies that motivate and engage them in thinking critically about content. Students and teachers can do a lot with the technology available on cell phones, but more sophisticated projects require more powerful technology and the right peripheral devices. And the success of it all depends on adequate infrastructure. In an active learning environment, where students are working on different activities at the same time, some individually, some in groups, some virtually, and some face-to-face, spaces need to be designed that make the right technology available to students when and how they need it.

Spatial Implications of Technology-Rich Learning

Steelcase Education Solutions completed a design research study in 2014 that involved observations and interviews at 16 schools, colleges, and universities throughout the United States. The intent of the study was to better understand the spatial implications of technology-rich learning approaches. Based on its study, the Steelcase Education research team has identified six key insights:

1. Person-to-person connections remain essential for successful learning.
Steelcase Education cites several studies suggesting that blended learning that combines online and face-to-face elements is more effective than either purely face-to-face or purely online learning. As described in Figure 2.1 earlier in this chapter, the best learning happens if best practices in pedagogy, technology, and space are considered equally when designing the learning experience.

2. Technology is supporting richer face-to-face interactions and higher-level cognitive learning.
Progressive educators are leveraging technology to create a more effective use of class time, forgoing mere information transfer in favor of more hands-on approaches to help students with advanced problem solving, communication, and collaboration activities. Spaces must also support students in hands-on activities and group work as well as be flexible enough to support varying activities and modes of learning.

3. Integrating technology into classrooms mandates flexibility and activity-based space planning.

Technology allows students to progress through material at different paces. As a result, multiple subjects can all be taught in the same room. Because blended learning changes the role of the educator to become more of a facilitator and coach, teaching is often done shoulder-to-shoulder, with multiple teachers acting as tutors and motivators.

4. Spatial boundaries are loosening.

Schools are increasingly recognizing the value of informal areas outside of classrooms where learning-based collaboration and reflection can occur. Inside the classroom as well, mobile furniture, moveable walls, and whiteboards can turn one learning environment into many. This level of flexibility helps students and teachers tailor learning experiences to the specific needs of students.

5. Spaces must be designed to capture and stream information.

With multimedia creation/consumption and video conferencing, many classrooms need to be equipped to not only view online content but create it as well. Video is also being used more and more as an evaluation tool for student-presented content or for demonstrating practical skills. Learners need ways to shut out distractions in self-directed learning environments for focused work. They also need flexible approaches to space division for different activities: group project work, group self-assessment, and receiving feedback from peers and grading from the teacher.

6. High-tech and low-tech will coexist.

Analog tools are often used in tandem with digital tools to support every facet of learning. Despite the growing presence of digital technology in today's classrooms, whiteboards, paper, and notebooks remain important tools for teaching and learning. For example, cognitive mapping research has shown that the physical process of writing helps people learn and recall information. Schools will continue to need spaces designed to support the parallel use of analog and digital tools.

Learning Spaces and Academic Achievement

Effective pedagogy and strategically designed spaces are, along with technology, the three essential components of a digital-age learning environment, an environment that supports active learning. Research on the role that learning spaces play in K–12 learning environments is just beginning, but we can draw some inferences from existing research on the kinds of learning experiences these flexible environments support.

Perhaps the most important component of academic learning is engagement.

In 2014, a team of Steelcase Education researchers, in collaboration with academic researchers in Canada and the United States, completed studies at four U.S. universities (Steelcase Education, 2014). A robust survey instrument titled the Active Learning Post-Occupancy Evaluation (AL-POE) was developed specifically for measuring the impact of classroom design on student engagement. This tool is widely recognized as a highly probable predictor of student success. To ensure adherence to the standards of academic research, the Steelcase Education team worked with third parties that included IRB (Institutional Review Board) research review protocol, researchers, and a statistician to analyze and report results.

> If learners engage in physics, they want to talk to engineers in the field.... Facilitating such expanded relationships requires a shift from vertical to horizontal classrooms—no longer the sage on the stage, teachers are learning alongside students, helping them actively construct their learning experiences and knowledge (Taylor & Parsons, 2011).

The results revealed that classrooms intentionally designed to support active learning increased student engagement on multiple measures as compared to traditional classrooms. In the universities studied, participants reported that the new classrooms improved active learning practices and had more positive impact on engagement compared to the old classrooms, with the majority of students rating the new classrooms better than the old. A large majority of students self-reported a moderate to exceptional increase in engagement (84%), ability to achieve a higher grade (72%), motivation to attend class (72%), and ability to be creative (77%). Almost all faculty members reported a moderate to exceptional increase in student engagement (98%), and all perceived a moderate to exceptional increase in students' ability to be creative (100%). A large majority of faculty reported a moderate to exceptional increase in students' ability to achieve a higher grade (68%), and a moderate to exceptional increase in students' motivation to attend class (88%).

Another study focusing on how certain spaces affect student engagement showed that creative spaces featuring flexibility, a unique atmosphere, and inspiring aesthetics led to more engagement. In this study—compiled in the *Use of Creative Space in Enhancing Students' Engagement* (Jankowska, 2007)—researchers found a direct connection between intentionally designed, flexible, active learning spaces and student engagement.

> The most commonly used adjectives throughout all the responses—such as: creative, positive, interactive, enjoyable, exciting, flexible, productive, engaging, involving, encouraging, inspiring, stimulating, fresh, functional, comfortable, relaxing, informal, personal, active—create a very positive and cohesive view of the [Creative Space], perceived as an excellent space for learning in a more unconventional way (p. 9).

Considerable research suggests the positive role that collaboration can play in academic achievement. We can thus infer that creating environments in which collaboration is easier and more productive will have a positive impact on learning. Another study (Dunleavy & Milton, 2009) describes three activities that students listed as important to their learning through interaction:

- Learning from each other and community members
- Connecting with mentors and experts
- Having more opportunities for interacting with each other

Educational research and theory provides substantial evidence for the effectiveness of a student-centered learning pedagogy. Learning environments that provide spaces for students to listen to experts when needed, to be free of distractions when they need to concentrate, and to learn from each other when they can, support students' academic development as well as their interest in learning.

REFLECT & DISCUSS

1. Research supports the efficacy of active learning over passive learning. In your experience, how do the results of the two approaches compare?

2. What are the major challenges to implementing an active approach to learning? How might these be overcome?

3. The amount of technology varies widely across communities. How does the level of technology in your classroom, school, or district affect student learning? What can be done to further leverage technology in your educational settings?

4. An ineffective teacher can still be ineffective in a well-designed learning space while an effective teacher can make the most of an imperfect environment. How are pedagogy and active learning environments connected?

CASE STUDY

Breaking the Norm
Orange County's The Academy Makes Space for All Learners

"Ben Franklin had a famous quote: 'Tell me and I forget, teach me and I may remember, involve me and I learn,'" says Anthony Saba, the head of school at The Academy in Santa Ana, California. "That's totally what we do here at The Academy. It's more than just holding something up in front of kids at the front of the class or showing them a PowerPoint. It's about involving them in their learning…involving them in their *own education*. That's where a learning space becomes a learning *experience*…and that's when the magic happens."

Figure 2.3: An aerial concept view of Orangewood's The Academy

The Academy is a college-preparatory public charter high school that will ultimately serve a student body of 480 foster, underserved, and community teens. The school welcomed its first class of 120 freshmen in August 2013 in its temporary quarters located on the building site of the school's new campus. As The Academy's 7.1 acres campus is built out, it will eventually include residential living for up to 80 foster teens. The attendance rate in that first year was 97%—one of the highest rates of any school in Orange County, California. Additionally, 50% of students finished the first year with a GPA of 3.0 or higher.

Saba attributes the school's early success to a fresh way of looking at how students learn.

"Most of us school administrators have gone through our lives experiencing only one form of education," says Saba. "But just because learning has been delivered the same basic way for all these years, doesn't mean that *that's* the best way to do things anymore. The Academy is engaging kids like no other school I've ever seen. But engagement through neat and engaging learning spaces coupled with phenomenal teachers is, unfortunately, not the traditional formula. That's why we have a 97% attendance record: Kids *really* want to learn this way. And our learning spaces go a long way in achieving that."

The Academy At-A-Glance

The Academy offers educationally underserved communities a new choice for the high school education of their teens. Future expansion of the campus will include on-site housing for those students who need a stable living environment in order for them to excel academically.

- 120 freshmen in August 2013.
- Each subsequent year, the school will add another freshmen class for a total student body of 480 teens.
- 80 foster students will reside on campus.

In the 2014–15 school year, The Academy had 13 teachers and 20 staff members. It will ultimately have 25 teachers and 35–40 staff members when fully staffed.

Seeing the Difference

Walking through the classrooms of The Academy, you can immediately notice a contrast from traditional school configurations. For one, there are no typical desks arranged in rows facing a teacher up in front of the class who is disseminating a lesson. You also notice flexible groupings of students who are collaborating with one another freely and with purpose.

"We not only teach collaboration in everything we do, but we assess on collaboration as well," explains Saba. "It's part of every student's grade in every single class: how well they can collaborate with one another. It's very hard to positively and effectively collaborate when seated side-by-side in rows, listening to lectures. They must collaborate with one another in every project, learning the essential interpersonal skills it takes to work in teams."

Figure 2.4: Students share ideas and concepts using whiteboards

The classrooms of The Academy feature Steelcase Verb tables and Node chairs so that the furniture can be quickly reconfigured to suit learning needs. The Node chairs have special arms specifically designed to accommodate tablet devices or laptops, and are in effect mini workstations. These mobile chairs allow students to easily form spontaneous learning groups to discuss a project or lesson with one another, or to congregate around the teacher for a teacher-driven discussion.

All students at The Academy have Toshiba laptops, while teachers have their own tablets, laptops, and smart projectors with interactive pens that allow them to navigate through content and draw graphs. Teachers also have document cameras. The school's engineering room has a 3D printer, and science labs feature microscopes with miniature LCD screens that are connected to laptops so that students can better carry out experiments. Even The Academy's health education classes have heart rate monitors that the students can strap on so that teachers can wirelessly monitor the bodily stats of each student.

The first two buildings on The Academy's new campus are scheduled to be completed by the summer of 2015. They will feature state-of-the-art interactive classrooms with cutting-edge technology for all students; an expansive, multi-functional student union; an extensive college and career resource center; a black box performing arts theatre; a learning commons area on each of the campus's three floors; and a new athletic gymnasium. There will also be couches in the school's lounge areas and open learning spaces so that students may work together, comfortably, in project teams or as individuals to complete work assignments.

Building the Skills Students Need to Succeed

As part of the New Tech Network—a nonprofit organization that works nationwide with schools, districts, and communities to develop innovative public schools—The Academy uses much of what the organization provides in terms of a rubric when teaching collaboration. At the end of every project, students must present their projects before a group composed of not just teachers but also outside community members who score and critique student presentations. Many of the same community members who assessed student presentations in The Academy's first year came to do the same in the following year since they were so impressed, seeing for themselves how the students grew in confidence and delivery.

"I, too, have personally seen how much our kids gave grown in mastering 21st century skills," Saba says. "Our flexible furniture and innovative learning spaces contribute to that. They have helped our curriculum to be wildly successful. Their flexibility makes every day in the classroom new and exciting. We also feature a 1:1 laptop environment, with every student having the technology they need to succeed academically. Combine this access to the latest technology with flexible active learning spaces that facilitate collaboration, then you've got an unbeatable formula for ensuring academic success."

The Academy's Best Practices

- STEAM (Science, Technology, Engineering, Art, and Math) curriculum
- Project-based learning
- Work-based learning
- Engineering and design pathways
- Small class sizes (approximately 20 students per class)
- Small student body (approximately 480 in grades 9–12)
- A Toshiba laptop for each student
- Caring staff focused on the "whole" student

The Academy actively assesses students' written and oral communication skills, as well as agency skills such as literacy and numeracy. According to Saba, having the right flexible and adaptable furniture configurations lends itself to all of this perfectly. Verb tables feature detachable, personal whiteboards so students can easily visualize learning concepts, share ideas with group mates, or write answers to a teacher's questions. This technology allows the teacher to instantly gauge the student's understanding and better assess outcomes.

With that said, furniture alone does not meet all of the many demands of modern education. The right teachers, the right tools, and plenty of support are also needed. Furniture, on its own, doesn't create an optimal learning environment; but it *can* support one. Even things like having chairs that swivel a little bit can make a big difference in learning.

"Back when I went to school, if the teacher had a situation where he or she needed to divert the class's attention, the class would have to pick up their chairs, and move them noisily into another configuration," says Saba. "With our Node chairs, however, students can move them quite effortlessly and quietly so that the flow of learning isn't disrupted. In this day and age, students struggle to maintain their attention…even a subtle movement back and forth can make a big difference on a student's attention span. When used in combination with great teaching and meaningful technology, the affect of the learning space can be profound."

Figure 2.5: A concept design of a communal, multi-use area

Serving the Underserved

The idea for The Academy began nearly ten years ago with Orangewood Children's Foundation, and it was spearheaded by philanthropists Susan Samueli and Sandi Jackson. Concerned about low graduation rates among high school teens in Orange County (including foster care teens served by Orangewood), Samueli and Jackson explored new educational opportunities for local high school students while researching best practices around the country. They rallied like-minded individuals and organizations from philanthropy, business, education, and child advocacy to join their efforts.

After spending nearly a decade meeting with experts, talking with foster youth, and researching intensively, Orangewood Children's Foundation realized it needed to build a school for *all* children, not just foster children. From these beginnings, The Academy was born.

The Mission of the Academy

To provide a transformational learning environment for foster, under-served, and community teens that offers consistency, stability, support, and a community in which to belong, thrive, and grow into responsible, independent adults.

"In this day and age, 21st-century skill building is not only about what students need to know, but *why* they need to know it," Saba says. "Students need to embody the skills that today's companies are screaming for. Not just ticking off answers to bubble tests, but a thorough mastering of how to work efficiently in dynamic teams; how to stand up and present your work with confidence; and how to work with and incorporate meaningful feedback. It's really hard to do any of those things when you've spent your school days sitting still and listening to lectures, simply regurgitating notes. *True* education is most powerful when students are in charge of their own learning—taking equity in their education—with this dynamic learning experience facilitated by skilled teachers well versed in new tools and new ways of engaging with their students. Future-thinking furniture configured in clever spaces is another arrow in our quiver, another way to bring our pedagogy to life."

CHAPTER 3

Reimagining the Classroom

Space matters. Most of us have home environments that not only meet our most basic needs but also suit our lifestyle and taste. The physical environment affects how we feel when we, or others, are in our home. Lighting, paint colors, and furniture can greatly influence the feel and functionality of a space. A home may be cozy with comfortable furniture, pillows, subdued colors, and low lighting. Such a space might provide a sense of relaxation. Or a home might be minimalist, without clutter or a lot of furniture, wall hangings, or knick knacks. Such a space could create a simple and undistracted feel.

Why should a classroom space be any different? The classroom environment is not neutral—it communicates what students will be doing in the classroom and what's important. A room with rows of fixed desks sends a very different message than a room with easily movable tables and chairs. If collaboration and other digital-age skills are important, students need a space that invites those skills. Busy educators know that the business of teaching and learning can be messy, chaotic, and often unpredictable. Many may struggle to find time to think about where students are going to sit or the type of lighting that is most conducive to learning. However, teachers can overcome time constraints, limited resources, and their many other commitments and adapt their classrooms to meet the requirements of digital-age teaching and learning.

The Impact of Effective Learning Spaces

Reenvisioning learning spaces empowers educators to employ best practice pedagogies that embed technology and make an impact on teaching and learning. Without a change in pedagogy or the way technology is used, new or redesigned classrooms will have no impact on student outcomes. It is critical that schools shift away from a classroom design that has the teacher as the center to a classroom that is focused on learners.

With a swift movement of furniture or the creation of spaces within spaces, a classroom can support collaboration, reflective thinking, peer mentoring, lectures, group projects, and more. Even at the same time, within one room, a classroom space can support students working on a variety of learning experiences or tasks in a more personalized, comfortable manner. Yes, one space can indeed combine caves, watering holes, campfires, and life!

By implementing the types of spaces most beneficial for teaching and learning, the configuration of those spaces, and the furnishings within those spaces, educators can create subtle and dramatic changes in classroom culture, interactions, and engagement. Imagine a classroom space that fits the learning instead of learning that fits the space!

 **YOUR TURN**

List the characteristics of your home environment that you appreciate on a daily basis. Draw connections to possible spaces in a classroom environment, either real or imagined.

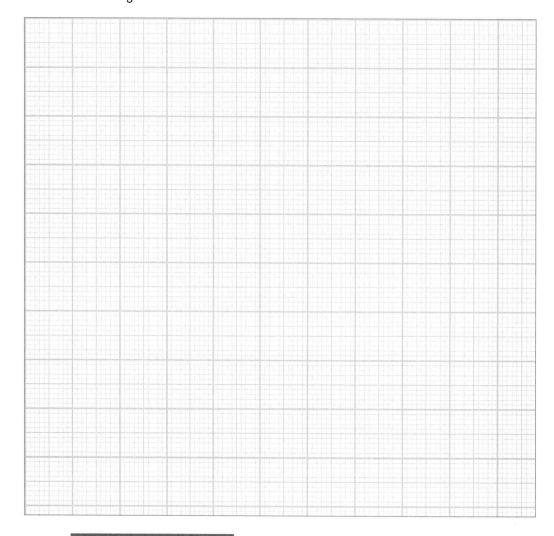

Home Work Spaces

Instructional models such as blended and flipped learning, and even old-fashioned home-work, extend student workspaces outside of the school building. Students often use laptops and tablets while lying on their beds or sprawled out on the floor. But should they? They work on math problems while watching videos on YouTube or write essays while listening to loud music on headphones. But should they?

Today's young people will undoubtedly say they can work well in these kinds of circumstances, that they're excellent multitaskers. But that is probably not the case (Paul, 2013). Just like at school, students need flexible spaces for working on school tasks, quiet places for solitary work and reflection, and collaborative spaces to work with others either face-to-face or virtually. They also need to learn how to make good decisions about how and where they work most productively.

Ergonomics is the design and arrangement of someone's work environment to fit the person. Without the benefit of ergonomics, people are forced into furniture or positions that are uncomfortable, which creates physical stresses. Or they are placed in an environment that may impact their hearing, vision, and general comfort and health. Ergonomics is an important consideration when designing a home work space. We are just beginning to understand the long-term physical effects of working with technology for long periods of time in unsuitable positions.

Similar to the hearing loss suffered by students who grew up listening to blaring music, students can experience serious physical problems that are traceable back to work habits developed in their youth. For example, in a recent study published in Surgical Technology International, back surgeon Kenneth Hansraj found that the average human looking down toward screens at a 60 degree angle places 60 pounds of force onto the cervical spine. The more time students are looking down at smartphones or other mobile devices, the more stress they are placing on their spines, leading to increased wear and tear (2014). Digital-age students need education in ergonomics, in understanding the kinds of furniture to use, and how to use it, as well as how to arrange the various components of a productive workspace. And the adults in their lives will need to model healthy ways to work.

A stimulating, student-centered classroom environment is one that engages learners on all levels—through sights, sounds, movement, emotions, and social interactions—and does not solely rely on a teacher to fill heads with lectures and one-way exchanges of knowledge. The learning environment should not only shake up learning for the student but also shake up teaching for the teacher. The space should encourage all students to take over the reins of their own learning, and grow their curiosity and expertise beyond their comfort zones. The space should allow them to connect concepts across disciplines in an atmosphere that builds collaboration, creativity, and communication skills in the context of developing deeper engagement with learning and content understanding.

Spaces within a Space

"From one class to the next, sometimes during the same class period, classrooms need change. Thus they should fluidly adapt to different teaching and learning preferences" (Steelcase Education, 2013). If a classroom provides choice of learning spaces and furniture, students can discover how their preferences, when considered in light of their productivity, can result in meaningful creative work, either by themselves, in pairs, or in groups.

Agile classrooms can best accommodate multiple activities. The same physical areas may need to support listening, performing, creating, collaborating, and thinking. Active learning spaces accommodate virtual learning experiences, multi-age learners, long-term project work, and students using a variety of devices. The singular classroom actually needs to be a flexible multipurpose room. All spaces must be both comfortable and inclusive for students with special needs. Educators must pay attention to the spaces between desks and tables, accessibility within a classroom, and furniture that can be easily adapted or moved.

A shift to active learning experiences implies that students are expected to move. Movement stimulates thinking. According to brain researcher David Sousa, physical activity increases the amount of oxygen in our blood, and this oxygen is related to enhanced learning and memory. (Sousa, 2012). Space and furniture can encourage students to easily move if they need to, while standing, swiveling in chairs, or walking around. Furniture, such as swivel stools, allow students to rock back and forth on a cylindrical stool, and ripple benches (see Ripple by Steelcase) cater to students who need to change position or who work best in a comfortable extended position.

Equipping the classroom with furniture and supplies that can be easily moved is essential for a redesign. For example, rolling whiteboards make it possible for students to quickly reconfigure a space for independent and collaborative work. Casters can be added to tables, chairs, and desks in classrooms that otherwise would not have rolling furniture. An ideal, intentionally designed active learning classroom has the following characteristics:

- Designed to maximize student access to and ownership of the learning environment
- Versatile, allowing for multiple uses, concurrently and consecutively
- Maintained continuously
- Future proofed to enable space to be revised and modified
- Able to support multiple types of learning experiences
- Zoned for sound and activity
- Designed for comfort and efficiency
- Information rich and technologically reliable
- Connected to the outdoors
- Spaces for optimal learning experiences

Spaces for Optimal Learning Experiences

Reflect back to the section Types of Active Learning Spaces in Chapter 2, and then consider spaces that would improve the classroom experience. Where could these spaces exist in the classroom you know so well? The following section looks at different classroom activities and provides an example of an effective environment for each learning experience.

Quiet Work

Students reading, writing, reflecting, or working independently benefit from a quiet space so that they can concentrate and do their best work. Some students just prefer to work alone. Even so, with a more personalized approach, all students may be conferencing with teachers more often. Quiet spaces are the "caves" and/or private or public alone spaces. For students who need a more private, alone space to concentrate, consider using dividers like mobile whiteboards and bookshelves to allow students to work independently with few distractions.

Designated quiet spaces in the classroom are another option, such as a three-walled space or a pop-up tent. According to Professor Stephen Heppell (2013), "three walls are enough … They offer a space for mutuality, for an intimacy of collaboration, for serious study and focused conversations, for peace and quiet sometimes, for focus, and of course, with always one side open and an eye line in, for safety too."

> A fifth-grade teacher allows students to read when they finish their work. However, she noticed that students who were trying to read became frustrated and annoyed by the distractions in the room. The class discussed this issue and decided to ask parents to build three-walled human-size cubbies where students could put pillows and retreat to for reading. A few parents procured wood, nails, and hammers and assembled three human-size reading cubbies, or "nooks" as they came to be called. The reading nooks are freestanding and can be moved. However, they currently line a back wall.

Small Group Work

Digital-age learning means extensive collaboration on projects and other small group activities. Peer-to-peer teaching and learning is critical for a successful outcome. Most professional workplaces have conference rooms or other spaces for collaboration, and classrooms should as well. These collaborative areas can include whiteboards, technology, and ready access to other materials that are necessary for the given project or activity. Sometimes another space may be used, such as a media center or makerspace. This is the "watering hole," or private/together space.

> A high school science class is doing a mechanical engineering project, as a way to build engineering and design skills. In small groups, students identify a problem to solve, come up with a solution, and design and prototype their machines. Thanks

to a flexible workspace with movable and adjustable tables, students can easily work on the small group project at their own pace: research on the tablets; ideate on whiteboards; consider solutions, oftentimes try out some form of the solutions in an open space; and sketch or use 3D modeling software. For prototyping, they head to the Maker Classroom, which is equipped with all the tools they need.

Large Group Work

Moving away from a teacher-centered, lecture-based approach still requires whole group discussions, lectures, presentations, and instructions as needed. In an active learning space, ideally there is no "front of the room" where the teacher stands or students present. Instead, any part of the room can be set up as a presentation area. Mobile tables and chairs are well suited for facilitating whole group discussions, presentations, or lectures. This is the "campfire" where stories are told and large-group discussions occur. With the right design, this public/together model can be easily and quickly modified.

A seventh-grade social studies class is learning about civil wars. Each of the five small groups has created a presentation demonstrating why the war occurred, sharing ideas on how the war could have been prevented, and relating their learning to gang activity in their own community. Each group presents in a different way. One group created a short film; another group scripted a play; another group created a "choose your own adventure" website; a fourth group planned a debate-style panel; and the fifth group created a multimedia presentation. Students share their products with peers in another class as well as with community activists. For the presentations, students fold and roll aside most of the tables. They stack most chairs, but leave some out for visiting community members. They also keep a few tables out for computers. All students gather in the open space. A computer and projector are set up by one of the large whiteboards; a small stage with scenery is set up on the other side of the room; and laptops and tablets are set out against two walls.

Classrooms can also extend beyond their four walls. Hallways, in-between spaces, libraries, and outdoor areas are potential extensions of the classroom. A classroom may even extend further by way of field studies, internships, and excursions into "life" beyond the school building.

 **YOUR TURN**

What types of learning experiences would benefit from a change to the space? Which types of spaces would you like to incorporate into your classroom? Use the following space to create sketches of the different types of classroom learning: quiet work, small group work, and large group work.

Classroom Furniture

Learning can happen anywhere, but learning happens *better* with the right classroom design. Research on learning shows that creativity and collaboration can be enhanced through the redesign of space. In the book *Make Space* (Doorley & Witthoft, 2012), the authors purport that the design of furniture enhances the ability of teams to collaborate.

When envisioning a classroom as an active learning space, keep in mind a few considerations so as to best accommodate student and classroom needs. These considerations include:

Comfort

Seating and classroom furniture/accessories should be designed for comfort and to allow for individual preferences.

- An active learning space should have places for students to sit and work for sustained periods of time.
- Comfort is different for everyone, and the type of seating may vary depending on the type of work students are doing, so offering a variety of seating and posture-support options (such as lounge seating and seat or stool heights) is ideal.
- Seating options should vary and can include wobbly stools, foam benches, bean bags, yoga balls, or plush carpets. If students are not using desks or tables, clipboards provide a good solution for a writing surface.
- Comfortable chairs should be selected.

Ergonomics

Ergonomics is a science concerned with designing and arranging things people use so that the people and things interact most efficiently (Merriam Webster, 2015).

- Consider furniture that will benefit growing students' spines, posture, and positions.
- Chairs should have lumbar support and armrests, and feature adjustable heights and positions.
- Ideally, some tables will have adjustable heights.

Flexibility

Learning spaces should allow for different types of classroom activities and be easily customizable.

- For an agile learning space, modular seating should be purchased or created so as to facilitate quick reconfiguration.
- Furniture should provide for multiple purposes. For example, a bookshelf might double as a standing workspace, or a mobile whiteboard might serve as a seat divider.

- Include some furniture that allows students to move, such as wobbly chairs.

Mobility

Furniture should be easily moved to allow for easy reconfiguration of the classroom.

- Tables should have the ability to be folded and easily rolled aside so as to create an open gathering space.
- Chairs, too, should be easily movable. Chairs that are light and can be stacked are ideal.
- Some workstations could include an attached desk and chairs on wheels.
- Swivel seats should allow students to turn to see each other for collaboration, and they should also provide students a way to release nervous energy so they can better focus on learning.

Durability

Strength and durability should be taken into account when repurposing existing furniture or selecting new pieces. Here are some things to consider.

- Furniture should be constructed to handle the heavy use of the school environment.
- Classroom furniture should be easy to care for; "wipeable" surfaces allow for easy cleaning.

 YOUR TURN

Think of the furniture in your current classroom, school, or district. Use the following table to assess individual pieces of furniture according to the aforementioned considerations. Rank the level of satisfaction within each category, with 1 being the least satisfactory and 5 being the most satisfactory. The first column is filled out as an example.

Item Name	student desk				
Comfort	2				
Ergonomics	3				
Flexibility	2				
Mobility	4				
Durability	5				

Furnishing Today's Classrooms

Companies, such as Steelcase, design and make furniture that accommodates active learning. For example, some rolling desks, such as the Node chair, have laptop storage and desktops that can be easily pushed aside to allow for easy entry and exit. They are lightweight and have wheels for mobility. Tables may fold and have whiteboard tops and wheels for mobility. Design39Campus in Poway, California, only purchases furniture that is multiuse and mobile. They worked with a furniture company to customize some of the furniture they use. For example, legs on tables were moved an additional eight inches apart so students would not have to bother with a table leg placed in between their legs. When a teacher at Design39Campus says "reset," students know they are to fold, roll, and stack furniture off to the side, and they are able to do so in seconds.

A Focus on Tables

Adjustable height and flip-top tables allow for flexible use of space. Flip-top tables can be easily stored when not in use to provide for more open space. Adjustable height tables allow students to be comfortable no matter if they prefer to stand or sit. Standing work-stations also have health and learning benefits. A 2014 study showed that with standing workstations, students increased their physical activity and caloric expenditure; experienced less stress on spinal structure; and showed improved academic successes. (Benden, Zhao, Jeffrey, Wendel, Blake, 2014)

If funding is limited, rectangular tables with folding legs are a versatile and inexpensive purchase. Mobility is key in making it possible to reconfigure tables for different types of activities that accommodate teams. This can be accomplished by arranging an area of the classroom with taller tables and adjustable-height tables. For students who prefer to stand, a podium is another option. Castors oncan be added to tables to help students move from collaborative groups to whole-group or independent work in a matter of minutes.

A Focus on Seats

When planning for seating, student physical stature and mobility abilities are important to keep in mind. Student preferences may also be considered, and a variety of chairs allow for those preferences. The same seat style for thirty students may not be desirable: Some students may prefer to sit on stools, exercise balls, or the floor. Rocking stools, such as the Steelcase Hokki, or exercise balls allow for active students to keep moving. Moreover, these seating types take up a small amount of classroom space. Stackable or folding chairs can be moved out of the way when needed. Casters on chairs help students to easily move around and keep others within their line of sight. Mobile chairs with attached desks that move to the side for easy desk entry are another option. Small hand-built wooden bleachers are a good choice for a stadium/tiered seating area for whole-group or small-group work.

With different bodies, different learning styles, and different kinds of work it makes sense to have a variety of seating options in a classroom—the more the better. Like other learning tools, conversations about the furniture are important. Teachers and students must agree on usage, turn-taking, and expectations.

 YOUR TURN

Sketch some examples of ideal furniture for your active learning space. What would be your ideal chair? What would be your ideal table? Use the following space to brainstorm ideas.

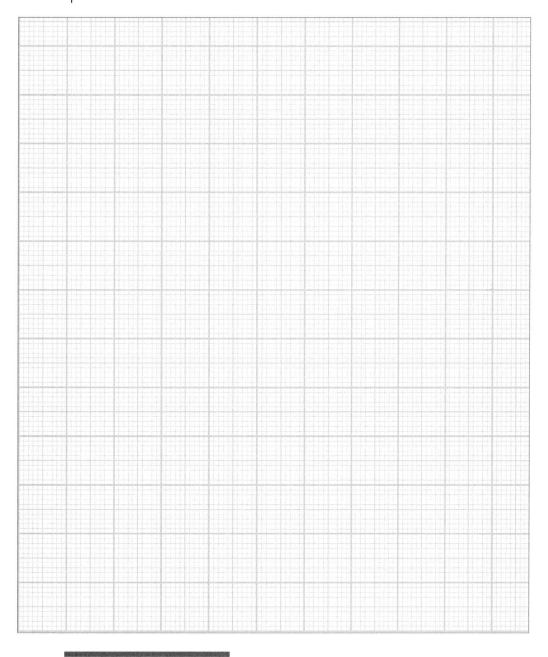

Accessorizing

Aside from rethinking furniture, other classroom features and products, both large and small, are worth exploring and can have a big effect on the efficiency and feel of a learning space.

Storage and Classroom Supplies

Storage containers, crates, and shelving can be used to divide space as well as hold a variety of supplies and equipment for student projects. Castors can make them easy to tuck away. A rolling cart stocked with project or art supplies can be easily moved to areas inside and outside of the classroom for sharing between classes. Discount furniture stores provide a wide variety of inexpensive storage solutions. For safe storage for mobile devices, consider carts, designated bookshelves, even hanging files in a locked file cabinet. All technology storage options should include a charging feature to make sure devices are ready for use when needed.

Personal Supplies Storage

Students bring stuff to school—books, pencils, jackets, lunches, mobile devices, and possibly a change of clothes for afterschool activities. Personal spaces may be at a desk with a cubby underneath, a backpack slung over a chair, or a locker. In a redesigned classroom, personal belongings are often kept out of the way of the learning space by way of hooks, cubbies, or bins. Pens, pencils, math, and art supplies can be shared and placed in designated locations.

Writable Surfaces

Some students like to write on desks, walls, doors, and windows—for the sense of audience, the collaborative nature of the activity, the exchange between writers, the rich colors, the personalization of large-scale writing, and more. Rolling whiteboards are one of the most versatile additions to any classroom. Whiteboards can be used for collaborative brainstorming or even as dividers to provide teams with more private space. Smaller double-sided whiteboards can be hooked onto the ends of tables for easy access. Tables with whiteboard tops allow space for personal ideation and expression, while vertical whiteboard surfaces (such as walls) make thinking visible to others while providing information persistence. Glass panels on the wall or white contact paper on tabletops can be used for writing notes.

Presentation or Teacher's Station

In active learning spaces, students and teachers may be sharing work, instructing small and large groups, or broadcasting videos. Rolling metal mobile teacher's stations are useful for moving the classroom focus around and projecting to different classroom areas. A cart may have a shelf for small projector storage, a laptop surface, and drawers for remote controls, pens, and other supplies. It may also include a removable tote bag.

LCD Display

Aside from a small mobile projector, an LCD display can be mounted on a wall so it's out of the way of learning. Likewise, this location minimizes distractions from bodies that might pass in front of the projector.

Display Space

Classroom walls can be maximized for the display of student work. Bulletin board strips can be attached to walls or hanging wires attached to the ceiling to provide ample room for showcasing work. High Tech High in San Diego was able to take advantage of its existing open ceiling architecture to create a variety of areas for showcasing student work.

Color

Research has shown that color contributes to students' ability to learn. Frank H. Mahnke in his book, *Color, Environment, and Human Response* (1996), suggests using cool colors to improve a student's ability to focus and warmer colors to stimulate creativity. Color-coding the different work zones in a classroom can help distinguish quiet areas from collaborative areas.

Lighting

Lighting, too, may influence students' learning. A research study, *Illuminating the Effects of Dynamic Lighting on Student Learning* (Mott et al., 2012), suggested the use of full spectrum lighting to improve focus. A study of 20,000 students showed test scores increased as much as 26% among students in classrooms filled with natural light (Chua, 2007). Lamps are another way to establish a more comfortable and natural learning environment. Even reducing the number of bulbs in fluorescent light fixtures can be helpful.

Each and every classroom should look different from one another. After all, no classroom, teacher, or student is exactly the same. Just some of the factors affecting a classroom design include grade level and subject matter, room size and shape, window size and placement (or the absence of windows), whether the classroom is shared by many teachers or is assigned to one teacher, and if students stay in the classroom most of the day or move between several classes throughout the day. And of course, individual teacher and student preferences also factor into the look of a learning space.

However, all classrooms start empty. Think about an empty classroom space, either an imaginary place or one you know well. Imagine it without furniture, with blank white walls, no lighting, and a swept floor. Perhaps the room has windows, perhaps not. If windows are there, they are uncovered.

YOUR TURN

In the blank space provided, draw a quick sketch of the empty space. Label assets that you want to capitalize on, including large walls or windows.

Now, imagine the students who inhabit that space. How would you like them to be learning? How would they be using the space? How are they moving through the space? What would students appreciate in a classroom?

Now, consolidate your learning and brainstorms about what constitutes your ideal learning space. In the space below, draw your final round of sketches considering furniture, accessories, and ideal areas for student learning. Feel free to try out new ideas. Remember this is just an ideation process to generate classroom design ideas for you and your students.

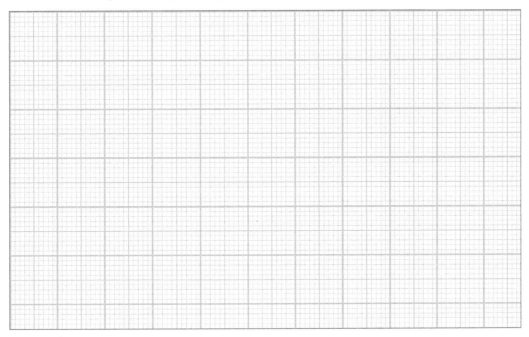

In the space below, make a list of what you want your students to be doing in your classroom. Now revisit your empty classroom and add some features to the space: perhaps desks, tables, and chairs, or something else.

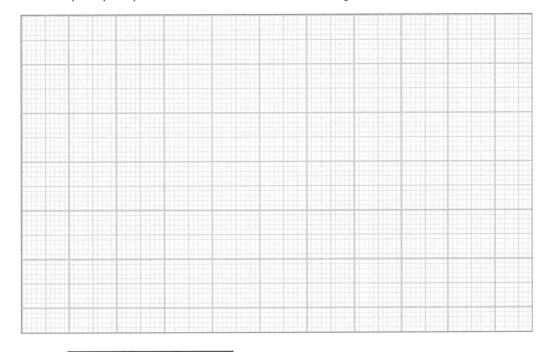

Daily Rituals

As you rethink classroom spaces, take time to observe daily classroom rituals. For example, at the beginning of the day, kindergarten classes often gather to sing songs and discuss the day ahead. A third grade class may be given activity choices for 45 minutes a day that could include reading, playing an educational game, working on homework or a project, or learning a language using an app. A middle school social studies teacher could have several daily newspapers delivered for students to read throughout the day. A high school science teacher may provide class time for students to work on engineering projects that interest them. Daily rituals are important when rethinking learning spaces.

 **YOUR TURN**

List your daily rituals in the space below. Consider how you would like a classroom space to best accommodate these rituals. Revisit your classroom sketch and integrate your rituals into your sketch.

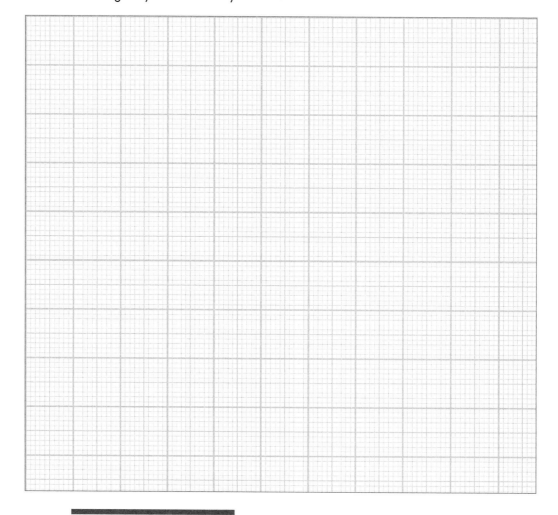

Teacher Research on Learning Spaces

At Hillbrook School in Northern California the media lab had been made obsolete by mobile devices. With support from Director of Technology, Bill Selak, and Center for Teaching Excellence Research Designer and Science Teacher, Ilsa Dohmen, educators redesigned the school's media lab into an Idea Lab (iLab). They shared their process and observations in a webinar entitled, Designing Agile Learning Spaces. An iLab is an active learning classroom where research is collected and ideas get piloted before they are implemented in the whole school. It's a space that is content agnostic; it can be used for things that can't be done in a more traditional classroom. The iLab is equipped with whiteboards, movable chairs and tables, window seats with soft cushions, and a couch in the corner. "Students love the lab," shares Dohmen, "compared to other learning spaces." The lab has a variety of seating options and tables, whiteboards, and a projector. After a class uses it, all furniture must be pushed to the side so the next class finds it "empty."

One of the guiding principles behind the iLab is to foster student choice; to allow students to set up the room and move around in it; and choose to manipulate their environment based on what they're doing. Dohmen recognizes that adults are used to honoring each other's work habits, but asks " how often do we honor those differences in students and children and how often do we give them the opportunity to even start to develop and discover what are the differences that work for them?"

For a research study of seventh and eighth grade students in a Language Arts class, the question posed was, "If you give students choice about their work space, will they be more productive?" To discover the answer to this question, a teacher at Hillbrook School set up the space herself, assigned seats, and gave a prompt about a novel that students had to respond to in ten minutes. After the exercise was complete, she gave out a new assignment. This time she set a timer for five minutes that allowed students to set up their own space. Students could do whatever they wanted to design the best space for silent writing. They then responded to a writing prompt for ten minutes. The freewrites from both exercises were assessed for word count and quality (claims and examples from the novel). They discovered that when the students created their own spaces, the results were significantly improved, with more words and higher quality responses. Teachers observed that when students had the opportunity to set up their own space, they didn't do anything crazy—just the act of asking students to create their own spaces gave them accountability and buy-in.

In another research study of a second-grade classroom, the objective was to understand the effect of movement on productivity. The hypothesis was that students in Steelcase Hokki stools could focus longer while getting their "wiggles" out. In one class, students used Hokki stools while doing as many problems as they could in five minutes. In the other class, students did the same worksheet, but on rigid stools. The two classes then switched.

Continued on next page

Continued from previous page

The results? Students in the wiggle stools completed significantly more problems than when seated on rigid stools.

Without being pushed, more and more teachers at Hillbrook School are asking for flexible furniture and are changing their learning spaces.

Future research could include studies on what would happen when the teacher:

- Allows students to stand or sit at the back of the classroom?
- Removes teacher-produced decorations?
- Says it's okay to stand up or fidget?
- Lets students work outside or sit on the floor?
- Asks students how they would change the space?
- Moves students' desks every day of the week?
- Gets rid of the teacher desk?
- Makes materials more accessible for students? (2015)

What are you waiting for? Individually or collectively, you can redesign a classroom space to accommodate digital-age learning experiences. Just imagine the possibilities.

 YOUR TURN

Now that you have ideas about classroom active learning spaces, tour other classrooms in your school or community. Identify spaces, furniture, and accessories that complement student learning. Make a list of ideas for your classroom space in the space below.

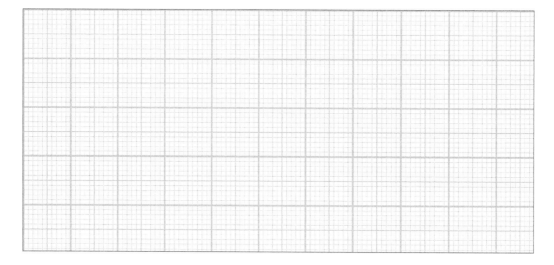

REFLECT & DISCUSS

1. Where do you do your best learning or work? What makes those space(s) effective?
2. Think of the learning spaces in your school or district. What types of types of student learning do they best accommodate?
3. Many learning space design ideas were presented in this chapter. Which design ideas seem the most feasible? What are the major obstacles to the ideas that don't seem feasible?

Redesigning Your Classroom

By Donna Teuber, Technology Integration Leader and Coach for Richland School District Two in Columbia, South Carolina

Educators don't need a large budget to redesign a classroom for active learning. One or two strategic purchases and some repurposing of existing furniture can transform classroom areas to allow for a variety of active learning experiences. Small adjustments to classroom layouts and reimagined classroom management procedures can positively impact student interactions, engagement, and learning as well. Successful redesign projects, like Room 17 in Oregon's Meriwether Lewis Elementary (described in the next case study) often happen gradually over the course of months or even years.

Once teachers determine the learning experiences that they want for students, it's essential to involve students in the process of redesigning the environment to best meet their needs (Bill, 2013). Engaging students in the redesign project is an empowering learning experience. Not only is their input about pain points and desires heard, but students engage in an authentic learning experience that can involve math skills such as measurement, scale drawing, and budgeting. In addition, they get practical experience with several digital-age skills that include problem solving, creativity, and collaboration. Design Thinking, an iterative methodology for creative problem solving, is ideal for this project.

A Process for Redesigning Your Classroom

Design Thinking, developed by the Institute of Design at Stanford University (the d.school) is a process for innovative thinking that involves five steps: Empathize, Define, Ideate, Prototype, and Test. Design Thinking lends itself well to student learning experiences where students select a problem and design a solution through ideation, collaboration, problem solving, and innovation. As you read this chapter, you'll see how the Design Thinking process aligns with the steps in a classroom redesign project.

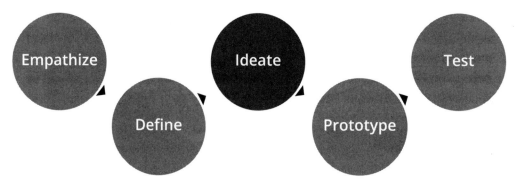

Figure 4.1: Design Thinking Process

Getting Started

The first step in designing an effective classroom is gathering information from students: the most important users of the learning space. Survey students to find out what makes them feel the most comfortable and productive, and ask them how they feel about the current environment. Survey items should provide the teacher and students with information on the kinds of features they feel would improve their ability to be successful.

Design Thinking Stage 1: Empathize

The Empathy stage of Design Thinking focuses on learning about the user. This may involve surveys, interviews, observations, and discussions to find out what matters to students in the classroom, what they might be bothered by in the current classroom environment, and what they'd like to see in the future.

 **YOUR TURN**

Take a moment to consider a current classroom from the perspective of a different user. This most likely will be a student. However, you could also choose a parent or an administrator. Once you've identified your user, list their feelings and issues with the space. If possible, interview a user for exact information.

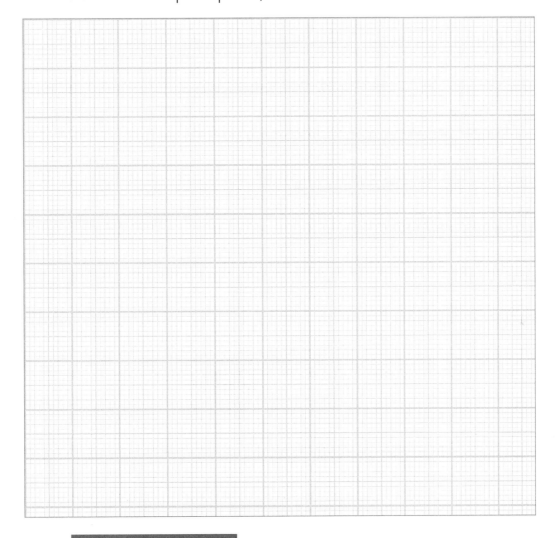

By turning the redesign into a learning experience, teachers and/or students might create a driving question that motivates students to consider their own needs, research best practices, come up with a plan, and implement the plan. Driving questions should help define the exact parameters of the projects and set the stage for success in the next steps of the process. A driving question might be: How can we redesign our classroom so it's the best environment for our learning?

Design Thinking Stage 2: Define

In the Define stage of Design Thinking, students use the information they collected in the Empathy stage to bring clarity and focus to the problem. By looking for patterns, considering context, and through explaining anomalies, students can create a problem statement that will drive the rest of the work (Stanford University Institute of Design, 2015).

Creating user personas is another way to define a project. This involves imagining a few different students and a teacher with varying needs and desires, and then describing how each person uses and feels about the current space, and what that person would like in a redesigned space. Before moving on to brainstorming your solutions, it's essential that the problem is clearly defined from the perspective of different users.

 **YOUR TURN**

Brainstorm a list of driving questions to help define the problems or critical issues that need to be addressed in your classroom redesign.

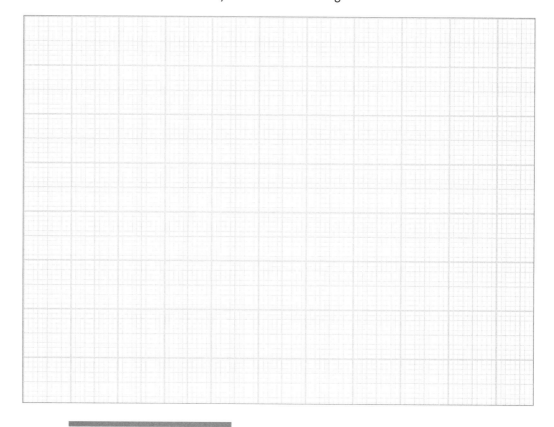

Brainstorming and Prototyping

Once a project is defined and needs are identified, participants are ready to propose ideas. Notosh (2015) includes a variety of activities to engage students in brainstorming at notosh.com/lab/come-up-with-great-ideas. One technique, called 100 Ideas Now, is designed to create lively discussion and help students come up with original ideas.

YOUR TURN

Design Thinking Stage 3: Ideate

In the ideation—or brainstorming—stage, students should be reminded not to judge any ideas. This is critical. Aided by activities such as brainstorming and researching inspirational materials, students concentrate on generating as many ideas as possible for a classroom redesign. These ideas provide the fodder for the next steps of the process: Prototype and Test (Stanford University Institute of Design at Stanford, n.d.).

Use Google Drawings or other computer graphics tools to draw a reimagined classroom. Many tools allow students to work collaboratively on designs in real time. Explore tools like Google Drawings and consider how you could use them for your design project. If possible, explore more than one tool to find a tool that will meet the needs of you and your students. Use the space below to record your thoughts on the program.

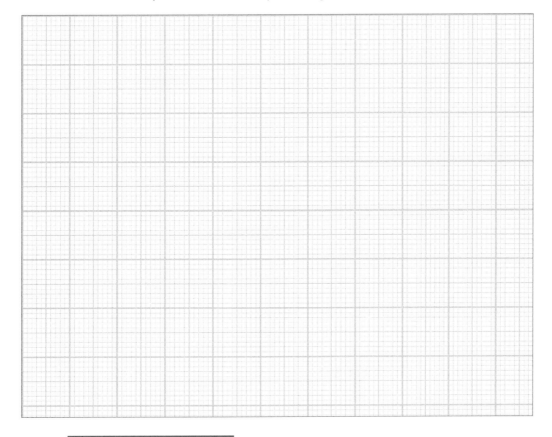

Design Thinking Stage 4: Prototype

Prototyping is a concept borrowed from the engineering field that is relevant for processes and designs. In this stage, students create artifacts that, through testing, will help them reach a final plan. Prototyping is a general term that can be applied to many different kinds of tools, and a task such as redesigning a classroom may need a few distinct prototypes.

After ideating, students can use whiteboards, Post-it notes, physical materials, and computer drawing programs to create a variety of prototypes for their solutions. Students can also use a variety of materials to create prototypes of their redesigned classroom. The Stanford d.school has a list of materials that can be used for creative prototyping at their website (dschool.stanford.edu/groups/k12/wiki/56 b69/Materials_List.html).

Consider the following steps to successful prototyping:

Step 1: Rapid Prototyping

Rapid prototyping is a technique that can be used to effectively redesign classroom space. Look at the prototype classroom designs developed by students and select something to implement immediately. If survey data shows that students need to have space for independent learning, use bookshelves or crates to make a private area. After implementing a new idea, observe and interview students to find out how they feel about the new space. Adjustments can be made if the initial experiment fails. This method allows the teacher to receive feedback before investing more time and funding on an idea.

Step 2: Large-Scale Prototyping

If everything goes well with the first step, continue to move forward. Add new features to the classroom, observe the classroom environment, and ask students for feedback about the changes. In Richland School District Two in Columbia, South Carolina, a high school technology coach at Westwood High School redesigned a classroom space into a makerspace by prototyping with large boxes to indicate where furniture would be placed. This allowed the technology coach to watch how students moved between zones before deciding on purchases. After watching the flow of students through the area, the technology coach purchased tables that would fit well in the new space.

Testing and Implementation

The next step is to go for a complete makeover. What would it look like if you moved out all existing items and reimagined the classroom for a thoroughly transformed learning experience? Empty out the room and bring back the items that fit into the learning experiences that students have designed. Remember that in an active learning space there is no longer a front of the room. When nonessential items are removed, more space is made available for a variety of classroom activities. By looking at the classroom through a new lens, students and teachers can redesign the classroom into a space that can transform the learning experience.

When the plan has been developed, students should assist with repurposing furniture, decorating, and organizing supplies. Set aside time after school or on the weekend for willing students to help with the project and plan an open house for parents when the redesign is complete.

Students in a Google Applications class at Kelly Mill Middle School in South Carolina's Richland School District Two learned business skills as they worked with their teacher to make the classroom more functional for their needs. At a certain point, they realized that they wanted to go bigger with their plan and acquired and redesigned a portable classroom into a "cloud classroom" using Google-themed colors, colorful bean bags, inexpensive decorations, and repurposed furniture. The initial efforts to change their existing space gave them important information about their needs, and they were successful with implementing the full plan when they acquired the new space.

> ### Design Thinking Stage 5: Test
>
> During the Test step of Design Thinking, designers collect feedback from users about the prototypes they have created. At this stage, users should first explore the process without explanation from the designers. Creating realistic scenarios and experiences for users with different components and variables provide the kind of information that planners can use to improve and refine their design (Stanford University Institute of Design, n.d.).

Getting buy-in from the local administration is important for the design to be successful. Policies that prohibit painting or moving furniture may need to be adjusted to allow for a learning space makeover. Students can also help with gaining support for the classroom redesign. Having students go through the design process allows them to take ownership of the project and lead to improved student engagement. As such, they can present their design to school leadership and explain why the changes will benefit their learning. Students can also contact business partners and parents to ask for materials and supplies. Organizations at the school may be willing to provide funding through existing fundraising efforts and endowments.

Iterating

Continue observing and testing the new classroom design even after implementation. Students and teachers should iterate back through the process, ideating once again to improve their designs and solutions based upon what they have learned during testing. The process continues until all stakeholders involved in the design project feel their classroom design accomplishes their goals. Even after a design has been implemented, the process can continue as students and teachers continue to make small adjustments to address problems and needs.

A practical example of a successful Design Thinking for developing a new school is presented in the case study of Design39Campus at the end of Chapter 5.

Repurposing Furniture

Furniture can be modified from current furniture or retired furniture from the school district. Table legs can be cut to make a low table for floor seating. Removing the storage spaces from underneath an old table can encourage sharing of materials. An old podium can become a standing desk. Wooden boxes can be made for nooks. And the list goes on. Beyond the obvious cost-saving benefits of adopting second-hand furniture, reusing and repurposing furniture models promotes sustainability and conservation principles to students, and also pushes them to act creatively and with resourcefulness.

ISTE Standards for Teachers

As teachers consider a move to active learning spaces, it is helpful to ground the process in standards for best practice. The ISTE Standards for Teachers (2015) define the skills, knowledge, and characteristics teachers need to demonstrate in our globally connected, digital world. As you read through the following standards, consider how they apply not just to technology but also to teaching in student-centered, active learning environments:

1. Facilitate and inspire student learning and creativity
   Teachers use their knowledge of subject matter, teaching and learning, and technology to facilitate experiences that advance student learning, creativity, and innovation in both face-to-face and virtual environments.
2. Design and develop digital age learning experiences and assessments
   Teachers design, develop, and evaluate authentic learning experiences and assessments incorporating contemporary tools and resources to maximize content learning in context and to develop the knowledge, skills, and attitudes identified in the ISTE Standards•S.
3. Model digital age work and learning
   Teachers exhibit knowledge, skills, and work processes representative of an innovative professional in a global and digital society.
4. Promote and model digital citizenship and responsibility
   Teachers understand local and global societal issues and responsibilities in an evolving digital culture and exhibit legal and ethical behavior in their professional practices.
5. Engage in professional growth and leadership
   Teachers continuously improve their professional practice, model lifelong learning, and exhibit leadership in their school and professional community by promoting and demonstrating the effective use of digital tools and resources.

Visit iste.org/standards for additional resources and information about the ISTE Standards•T.

A school media specialist in Columbia, South Carolina, repurposed her old library chairs into modern stools by removing the backs, painting the frames, and reupholstering the seats with new fabric. Students painted the tops of wooden library tables with whiteboard paint and added casters for better mobility.

Prior to updating existing furniture and making new purchases, teachers might work with the school's art teacher to develop a color scheme for the room. Color can be added through paint, fabric, and accessories. Paint stores provide a variety of color palettes and design ideas to help with the selection of colors that support the desired learning environment for each work zone.

> Many crafty suggestions and plans can be found in the book *Make Space: How to Set the Stage for Creative Collaboration*. For example, you can learn how to create your own foam cubes and movable walls (Doorley & Witthoft, 2012).

A teacher at Richland School District Two's Summit Parkway Middle School involved students in the design process and was able to turn her media center into an active learning space. Students worked with her to create a makerspace by brainstorming their needs and developing computer designs for the space. After creating a plan, they pitched their idea to the district administration to receive support for painting walls and repurposing furniture. Students participated in all stages of the redesign and gained valuable entrepreneurial skills (2014).

Overcoming Challenges

When redesigning classroom space for learning, teachers will face challenges. Classroom space and funding are limited. There is also fear that students will be off-task if they're not visible to the teacher at all times. These challenges can be overcome by thinking differently about the use of space. Letting go of some control is key to getting started with transforming a classroom for active and flexible learning. Following are some common challenges and how to address them.

Buy-In from Leadership

Teachers can work with colleagues and students to develop a plan that will be pitched to school leadership. Include research studies and student feedback about learning to provide a convincing argument for redesigning classrooms. Present leadership with a reasonable budget and explain the process for moving forward with the plan.

Time

Time for planning, prototyping, repurposing and purchasing items, and evaluating the redesign is needed. Involving students in the design and creation of the space, and making the creation of the space their learning experience, may take more time than you usually spend on classroom projects, but consider it time well spent. Successful redesign projects can improve student teacher relationships and foster a shared sense of ownership over the space, setting the stage for more balanced and productive learning environments.

Fear

Fear can become a barrier to creating a classroom environment that allows for active learning. Teachers considering a transition to student-centered learning may voice concerns that classroom management will be more difficult when students are moving between activities and collaborating in teams. By developing classroom procedures that set the new classroom up for success, teachers will feel more comfortable about giving up the control of teaching from the front of the classroom. Teachers in well-managed classrooms incorporate assessment strategies with clear expectations for classroom behavior and the work that students need to accomplish. Learn more about management in the Managing an Active Learning Space section.

Parent Concerns

Parents may be concerned about the redesign and wonder if the environment will be conducive to assessments and independent work. Counter this concern by offering an open house and asking students to demonstrate how they work in the space. Showcase student learning through blogs, electronic newsletters, and social media.

 **YOUR TURN**

Find other teachers who have redesigned their learning spaces. Ask them about their process. What steps did they follow? How were they able to involve students? In addition, find out strategies they used to overcome any obstacles to a successful redesign, including those listed previously. Record your findings below.

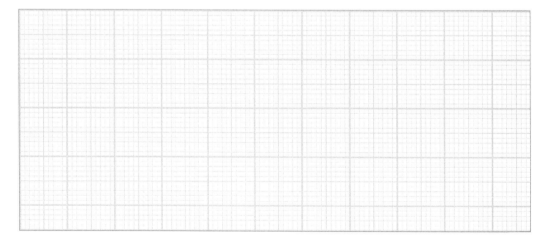

PLANNING GUIDE

The following planning guide can assist you as you transform a classroom space:

- ❏ Observe how students and teachers currently work in the space and interview them to find out which type of environment works best for them. Think about extreme users—the most active students and the quietest students—and evaluate how the change might impact their work.

- ❏ Research best practices for flexible learning environments.

- ❏ Survey students to find out about their learning styles and preferences.

- ❏ Work with students to brainstorm ideas for the space based on their learning needs.

- ❏ Involve students in creating a prototype of the redesigned classroom using a computer drawing program or craft materials.

- ❏ Decide on the purchases that will provide the most benefit within a reasonable budget.

- ❏ Take advantage of design advice and assistance from an art teacher or furniture supply store designer.

- ❏ Get buy-in from the school administration by creating a budget and timeline for implementation.

- ❏ Communicate the plan to parents and ask parents for assistance.

- ❏ After developing a prototype, ask students to pick the most promising and feasible ideas to implement immediately.

- ❏ Involve students in repurposing existing furniture and assisting with fundraising and asking for donations.

- ❏ Observe and refine ideas based on the reactions from the first rapid prototype.

- ❏ Continue to introduce new features. Observe and get feedback on each change.

- ❏ Host an open house for parents to see how their children are working in the new space.

All learners deserve a space that can be customized to meet individual learning needs. When students are given opportunities to make decisions and provide a variety of seating options, they learn to make choices that best suit them, discovering that they may prefer to stand, wobble in their seat, or sit on the floor. Fortunately, preferences can be expressed in an active learning space.

To accommodate a variety of learning preferences and physical needs, teachers and students can redefine how traditional classroom space is used. By involving students in the design process and looking at ways to maximize a small budget and existing resources, teachers can reinvent the classroom into a dynamic space that engages students in learning.

 REFLECT & DISCUSS

1. New or old? In your opinion, what are the pros and cons of repurposing second-hand furniture or buying completely new furniture for a classroom space?
2. Have you ever used the Design Thinking process before? If so, for what type of project? How do you think it would work with a classroom redesign?
3. Involving students is essential to creating shared ownership, but can come with challenges. What are these challenges?
4. What steps can you take to generate buy-in for your redesign project from different stakeholders including students, parent, and administrators?

Managing an Active Learning Space

As mentioned, fear can be an intimidating obstacle for teachers considering a transition to a more active learning space. For example, some teachers—citing off-task conversations or distractibility when students sit in groups—might prefer to keep desks in rows facing the front. Others might be wary about losing track of learners and their progress when working on diverse tasks in spaces scattered throughout a classroom or school. Without doubt, teachers are confronted with giving up a certain amount of control when they allow students to move freely about the room, make decisions about where and how they learn, and provide access to technology.

However, educators should not be fearful of what, in the end, is a good thing: taking full advantage of spaces in an effort to accommodate every learner and every learning activity. What's more, personalizing learning experiences for individual students is not a new idea. Many teachers may already have an intricate understanding of the nuances of managing an active learning approach, and it turns out that many of the strategies that apply to managing learning in the digital age also apply to managing active learning spaces. Consider the following management ideas that may not seem all that new, and note how they apply to managing an active learning space.

Give Students a Voice

The learning space belongs just as much to students as it does to a teacher. Think about how you can involve students in the design of the space. Also, give them a role in developing routines and guidelines that fit the environment. Involving students in these defining steps can increase student buy-in and ownership over the space. Instead of feeling like something is being pushed on them, they will be co-creators: fully invested in making the new space work.

Plan and Pre-teach Procedures and Skills

Underneath a seemingly free learning environment is often a carefully crafted structure governing how the space functions. With a new learning environment comes a need for a whole new set of procedures. From the overarching questions (How will students choose spaces appropriate to learning activities?) to the fine details (How will technology be charged and ready for use?), any time spent planning how the new environment will operate is useful.

Teaching and consistently reinforcing these routines and procedures is also essential. While it may take more time than you'd like in the first weeks of school, it will pay off and save time in the long run. In addition, consider that working efficiently in new spaces will require new skills. For example, direct instruction in and assessment of characteristics of skills such as effective collaboration and communication will improve the quality of learning in your room. Lagging skills are often untaught skills.

Set High Expectations

Many times, the only thing holding our learners back can be our expectations. When high, yet fair, expectations for student behavior in the learning environment are clearly defined, students will often rise to meet them. When the expectations are not met, teachers must hold students accountable. In Ms. Kennedy's classroom at Lewis Elementary School, when students make poor decisions about where to sit, they lose that privilege for a week. (For more details, see the Case Study that concludes this chapter.) A similar system of natural consequences can go a long way toward ensuring positive behavior in your new space.

Likewise, set high expectations for student work. These expectations should be clear, reasonable, and individualized as much as possible. If students are supported through the

Continued on next page

Continued from previous page

process, high expectations for student learning will help students be more efficient in the learning space.

Encourage Student Metacognition

Active learning spaces require students to make ongoing decisions about which spaces match their specific needs and individual preferences. Given the right amount of support and practice in how to reflect and monitor their performance, students will gradually develop their self-management skills. Not only is this a benefit to your students personally, but as students take control of their own decisions, your space can actually begin to manage itself.

Use Formative Assessments

Constant formative assessments—including, among others, audio, visual, and text observational notes; skill and project checklists; self-reflection and peer feedback; mini-conferences; and exit tickets—can help students stay focused on learning projects and goals. With increased information on student progress, you'll likely feel aware of individual student progress and needs, even though they are engaged in a wide variety of activities in a wide variety of spaces. Connecting these assessments to space as much as possible will inform the decisions you and your students make about which spaces are best for which learners and activities.

Share Your Space

Inviting visitors into the room to observe your space and all of the great learning that happens there can be a powerful way to convince others of the many benefits of active learning spaces. It can also generate student pride in their space. With pride comes a greater sense of respect, a respect that will encourage students to maintain and care for the space and those in it.

Active classrooms will have students all over the room while they engage in different activities. There is no way to monitor students without transitioning to a more mobile teaching style. Get up and move around. Listen in on collaborative sessions, glance at screens and check in with students during independent study. This type of passive supervision communicates a clear message that you take an interest in students and their learning, and your students will appreciate your active engagement. In addition, student behavior may improve just because they know you're always up and about.

Flexibility has been and will continue to be mentioned throughout this book as a key ingredient for successful active learning spaces. It should also be considered a key ingredient for managing an active learning space. Once created, your design should not be considered set in stone. As problems arise—and they will—with either certain spaces or certain procedures or guidelines, be flexible as you work with students to find creative solutions in this learning space that you and your students maintain together.

Active learning itself can actually be an excellent tool for classroom management. Given more control over their own learning and learning spaces, student engagement can improve. With increased engagement, teachers can expect less behavior issues. Sure, there will be bumps along the way. But don't let fear get in the way of establishing an active learning space.

 **CASE STUDY**

A Place for Every Learner and Learning Activity
Meriwether Lewis Elementary: Room 17's Learning Space

Upon walking into Room 17 of Meriwether Lewis Elementary in Portland, Oregon, it's immediately obvious that the space has been purposefully designed for the unique characteristics of each individual student and a wide variety of activities involved in the learning process. The third grade students are smiling, excited about their classroom and their learning. They are busy attending to instruction, sharing and collaborating with peers, and working independently. They are monitoring their own learning, and making decisions about which spaces best fit their current requirements.

Figure 4.2: Room 17's variety of spaces accommodate all learners and learning activities.

You'd think in a room with 25 students that a certain degree of messiness would be a given. But Room 17 is shockingly organized and uncluttered. Every pencil is sharpened, and all the supplies are ready for use in easily accessible communal areas. Asus Chromebooks are either charging in their stations or in use by students. What's more, the space appears to care for itself—as students leave at the end of a busy afternoon, everything is put back in place and made ready for the next day.

Through it all, the classroom teacher, Pamela Kennedy, glides around the room. She checks in with individuals and groups and engages students with her energy, demeanor, and attention. She is clearly a guide. And everything in the room—from the spaces to the intricate routines and procedures—was intentionally designed by Ms. Kennedy to enhance the learning experience for each and every student in her room.

At a Glance:

- School: Lewis Elementary
- Location: Portland, Oregon
- Teacher: Pamela Kennedy
- Classroom grade: 3rd grade
- Number of students: 25
- Website: https://mskennedy17.wordpress.com
- Twitter feed: @PamelaKennedy17

The Space

Ms. Kennedy was a pen-and-ink illustrator and stay-at-home mom. Her transition into teaching started with volunteering in her son's classrooms. She then became an educational assistant and para-educator with the opportunity to observe teaching and learning in a variety of learning spaces. Upon becoming a certified teacher, she finally got the opportunity to design her own space. Ms. Kennedy describes her current classroom, Room 17, as "a place where an optimistic person has the ability to instill a genuine love of learning." To that end, she provides spaces that accommodate not only many different learning activities but also the unique learning styles and needs of all the students.

"Creativity, comfort, and bold design are elements I now embrace in my classroom. Over the years, I just keep removing any physical and social barriers that inhibit instruction, movement, and interaction. Students now have the flexibility to customize their environment, to meet their unique learning styles and personal preferences. Room 17 fluidly evolves and takes shape as needed for lessons and activities of the moment."

Hokki stools and Zuma chairs

Not one single traditional school chair exists in Room 17. Instead, when students are sitting they sit in chairs that allow for a range of movement and learning styles. Hokki stools provide a gentle rocking motion that lets students keep moving while sitting still. The cantilever Zuma chairs, ergonomically shaped, appeal to students who prefer a backrest. Both seating options are light enough to be easily moved around the classroom and can be lifted onto a table for easy cleaning.

Figure 4.3: Students at work sitting on Hokki stools

Node chairs

The attached work area, the sturdy casters, and ability to swivel make the Node chair a popular seating option in Room 17. The chairs' mobility allows for all types of classroom learning. For group work, they can be arranged into collaborative pods. During instructional time, they can be wheeled to face the front. And for times requiring independent focus, they can be rotated to create private work areas.

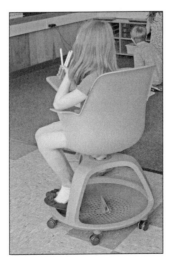

Figure 4.4: A Node chair arranged to promote focus

High table

Sitting in any chair can be hard for extended periods of time. A high table provides students a little bit more freedom of movement to get their work done and collaborate while standing up.

Low table

Students can choose to sit on carpet squares surrounding a low table covered with IdeaPaint, which transforms the table top into a whiteboard. Dry erase markers in hand, students are encouraged to collaborate and share their thinking. Ms. Kennedy can quickly "get a clear overview of students' thought processes and work" and "provide immediate feedback, [that is] so important in formative assessment."

Figure 4.5: The podium allows students to focus on their work while standing.

Podium

According to Ms. Kennedy, "It's always a good idea to have an individual standing workstation designed for one learner." During writing lessons, students really appreciate the location of the podium because it provides a clear view of a word wall.

Rug area

Most elementary classrooms include a community area for instruction, presentation, and discussion. Room 17 is no different. However, what is impressive is how purposefully the space was designed. A teacher workstation with computer and document camera, the ceiling-mounted projector, the white board, and the neat, simple, accessible displays make the gathering space particularly usable in Room 17. Students not only have a spot to gather as an entire class, they also have a spot that grants all students a front row seat to that day's presentation.

Reading cubbies

Ms. Kennedy has moved the coat racks into the hallway where backpacks, coats, and lunches remain throughout the day. In the absence of all this clutter, the extra space allows for three simple, yet functional cubbies that can each fit two students. Students can climb into the confined spaces to find that short moment for reading a book or having a discussion with a friend.

Reading bleachers

A two-tiered bench constructed in the corner is a natural spot for students to read as a group, meet with a book group, or collaborate on work. Although it takes up little actual floor space, the bleachers are a comfortable place for learners to gather.

Technology

When not in use, neatly arranged Chromebooks charge on a low counter in the corner of the room. Much of the time, however, the Chromebooks are in the hands of students who leverage technology for learning in all areas of the room.

The Process

Ms. Kennedy insists that breaking away from a traditional classroom and establishing an environment suited to the personalized needs of each learner is not difficult to do, it's just the outcome of a deliberate process. She describes a classroom as "just your basic square. You just need to be thoughtful about what you put in it."

When Ms. Kennedy moved from teaching kindergarten to third grade, she inherited not only the classroom but also all of its contents. Her first task was to remove all the unnecessary items from the classroom. About all that met Ms. Kennedy's approval was the "bank of large, beautiful windows" looking out onto the school garden. According to Ms. Kennedy (a self-described minimalist):

"I removed everything from the room and conducted an inventory of what I felt was necessary. For example, five file cabinets were whittled down to one. Dozen-upon-dozens of random plastic containers were recycled. Mismatched circular tables and single desks were replaced with tables for six students."

With a clean slate, Ms. Kennedy started the process of reinventing her classroom from the ground up. Ms. Kennedy wanted the Room 17 learning space to "be highly structured, uncluttered, and organized—transformed from the institutional space it was in the fifties."

Given the very finite resources available in a public school budget, Ms. Kennedy had to be resourceful when setting up and furnishing Room 17. Many of the contents of the room make it appear fresh but were actually gathered at little or no cost. The stand-up table was donated, the low dry-erase table was picked up on clearance, and a parent of a former student constructed the podium. Ms. Kennedy's handy husband, Craig, built the reading bleachers and cubbies, and moved the coat racks into the hallway.

A redesign this thorough is hard to accomplish without at least some funding, but Ms. Kennedy has been resourceful in this regard as well. Ms. Kennedy has found success with DonorsChoose.org, a website connecting public school teachers and their projects with donations. Ms. Kennedy has figured out how to create successful grant applications, and she focuses on specific regional grants and matching donations from corporations to avoid taxing the financial resources of her school and personal community. Now Ms. Kennedy is passing on her expertise in utilizing the DonorsChoose.org site to her colleagues and other educators. The opportunities for funding are out there, it's just a matter being creative in finding them.

> Ms. Kennedy pays attention to the small details because highly organized spaces bring a pride of ownership and sense of communal care to the environment. A local paint store matched the wood stain from the room so the reading cubbies and the bleacher fit right in. And the wire book baskets—acquired from the gym teacher—provide a consistent look through the room.

The Routines

Ms. Kennedy has brought as much intentionality to the process of adopting routines and procedures for the active learning classroom as she has to designing the spaces. At first glance, given the amount of freedom that students have to move about, class time might appear to be disordered or chaotic. However, supporting this "busyness" is a clearly defined structure that the students respect and, more importantly, appreciate.

Ms. Kennedy lays the foundation for a positive learning climate with the routines that begin the day and end it. She states, "Each morning…I kneel down in the doorway of Room 17 and greet each student with a handshake or hug. It is my way of expressing how happy I am to see them and how important it is that they came to school.…In the afternoon, students are dismissed the same way, and I thank them for a great day of learning and let them know I look forward to seeing them the next school day."

The students who learn in Room 17 are required to "assume responsibility for gathering materials" and "know there is a place for everything." Singing during transition and cleanup times energizes the classroom and keeps the learning momentum moving into the next learning activity. Ms. Kennedy utilizes kindness, recognition, and redirection to manage students. When students need redirection during mini-lessons, she invites them to sit in her "zone of proximity," allowing them to quickly refocus their attention on the learning at hand without feeling disciplined.

Ms. Kennedy believes each week is a new week. Accordingly, students start each Monday in a new seat. She explains, "Each Friday, after our room cleaning and class meeting, students are randomly selected to choose their spot for the upcoming week. Students opt for different work environments around the class. They learn to 'choose wisely' or they will lose the privilege for the week." Students in Room 17 take decisions about their learning seriously, oftentimes choosing a seat based on their learning needs as opposed to where their friends are sitting. Regardless, students are given so much choice about where and how they work within any given learning activity that they do not feel limited by their seat assignments.

Figure 4.6: Small details like individual name cards and pencil holders make Room 17 an inviting place for students.

In Room 17, the teacher and students are energized and engaged, moving freely yet productively around the room while actively making smart choices about how, where, and what they learn. The unique qualities of each student are identified while spaces and routines are designed with the best interests of students in mind. When asked, students appreciate the variety of spaces in the room—but above all—they appreciate Ms. Kennedy, the one who created the environment that makes their third grade experience engaging, fun, and focused on learning.

CHAPTER

5

Schools for the Future

Space is the blank canvas where anything can happen. Space is the third component, along with pedagogy and technology, of an active learning environment. Space is a clean slate (or not-so clean slate, depending) that awaits an educator's unique mark. Space can be the stage where dramatic acts of learning can occur. According to the authors of the book *Make Space*, "Space is the body language of an organization, with its own grammar that can be tweaked to bolster desirable habits" (Doorley & Witthoft, 2012).

Space can be most anything you want it to be. And that is both the challenge and the opportunity. Although the effectiveness of student learning in the classroom depends primarily on the teacher, a school building can either facilitate or inhibit an active learning pedagogy. Some learning spaces lend themselves to collaboration, creativity, and communication; others leave students feeling isolated and confine them to rote learning with out-of-date content and materials. A well-designed physical space can inspire teachers to be creative and design learning experiences that take full advantage of active learning opportunities.

Digital-Age School Architecture

If you are fortunate enough to be designing a new school or modifying an existing structure, you have the opportunity to think about the school space in creative ways such that you can maximize its impact on student learning, particularly the interactions among students and between students and teachers.

Several features contribute to the overall atmosphere of a school. McCrea (*Campus Technology*, 2012) recommends an overall physical shell with high ceilings, controlled lighting, and open-room layouts. Light is an important component of a digital-age school. Students and other school personnel spend a good portion of their time inside a school building, particularly in geographic regions with extreme weather conditions, and there is evidence that "there are direct connections between our physiological well-being as humans and the amount of daylight we get" (Nair et al., 2013, p. 151). One of the most important modifications that can be made to an existing school is the removal of walls and barriers, and the addition of windows and doors to let in more light (p. 92).

Natural light isn't always the best environment, however. Teachers, and even students, need to be able to control the lighting. At times they might need bright lighting for boisterous activities, or they may need dim lighting for viewing media or for facilitating quiet thinking in a private place.

Connections with the outdoors are also important in a learning environment. Students of all ages need areas for vigorous play and socializing, and a well-designed school uses its outdoor spaces whenever possible to enhance academic learning. "[O]utdoor areas such as learning terraces, kitchen gardens, shaded reading areas, natural creeks and other water features, nature trails, and playfields" provide opportunities to apply content learning to the real world. When weather permits, outdoor spaces can provide good options for learning activities that are too big, too messy, or too noisy for indoors (Nair et al., 2013, p. 111).

Storage is another important consideration when designing learning spaces, particularly where students by necessity move from room to room and do not stay in one space for most of the day. Storage is also critical for providing students with the materials they need for creative work. Doorley and Witthoft recommend allotting at least 30% of a school's space for storage and suggest leasing off-site spaces for seasonal items. Storage areas, according to these authors, should be transparent so that stored items are visible and don't fade from people's minds and go unused (2012).

Researchers and designers of learning environments are often at odds over whether the learner should adapt to the learning environment or whether the learning environment should adapt to the learner. This is the wrong question. Instead, a better question is: "How does the environment shape the learner and, in turn, how does the learner influence the learning environment?" (Lippman, 2010)

Traditional secondary schools place lockers in hallways or areas separate from the classrooms. This design can cause crowding and allow for bullying out of the sight of supervising adults. To promote a safe school environment, individual storage, such as lockers, should be placed in areas of passive supervision. In addition, Nair and his colleagues recommend building lockers out of materials other than metal, which is noisy and easily bent (2013).

Another way in which the architecture of a school can contribute to student learning is by specifically designing features of the school to support the academic curriculum. For example, leaving architectural or engineering systems visible can give students a real life illustration of concepts they are studying in their math or science classes, which helps students see the practical applications of what they are learning in the abstract (Nair et al., 2013). Other possible uses of this strategy could be the identification of landscaping elements, geometric designs, and historical artifacts. The well-designed or redesigned school can serve as a 3D textbook that demonstrates the connections between the abstract and the concrete—actual concrete, in some cases!

In most communities, schools are more than just places where students go to learn math and history—they are centers of community activity. Sports, music, and drama events attract parents, former students, and other community members. Educators use school facilities to meet with community partners, and many schools are used by community organizations such as Scouts and 4H clubs for meetings outside of regular school hours. Making a school a warm and welcoming place for the community can create a supportive environment that pays off with parent support for the classroom, not to mention voter support for school bonds and levies.

One way to welcome the community into the school is by paying close attention to the school's entryway. The installation of seemingly minor features, such as a canopy or roof just outside the main entrance so that visitors can get out of the weather for last-minute exchanges with their children or to

> ## ISTE Essential Condition: Engaged Communities
>
> "Leaders and educators develop and maintain partnerships and collaboration within the community to support and fund the use of ICT and digital learning resources."
>
> ISTE holds that establishing community buy-in is a prerequisite for successful technology integration. Establishing community support for a transition to active learning and the creation of active learning spaces is also essential. Dedicating on campus spaces for community members to gather, such as welcoming entryways and community rooms, can give community members a close-up view of the transformational impact technology and learning spaces are having on student learning.

make preparations to go inside, demonstrates consideration for the patrons of the school. Another suggestion is to designate a specific space near the entrance where community members can store their belongings, have meetings, make phone calls, and access the internet (Nair et al., 2013).

Because the entrance to a school is a visitor's introduction to the school, its design should communicate the school's mission, culture, and values. Display areas for student work can highlight the importance of academic achievement. Nair and his colleagues remind us, however, that "The best display of student learning is active learning itself. On walking into the school, the community is able to see the core business of the school: students engaged in meaningful activities" (2013). If student work areas are not visible from the entryway, a wall-mounted flat screen TV can be used to cycle through important school information and display images and videos of student learning in progress.

 **YOUR TURN**

Sketch or diagram your ideal entryway. Consider what you want students, staff, and community members to be doing in the space. Think about the displays.

What types of information or artifacts will immediately communicate your school's mission and values?

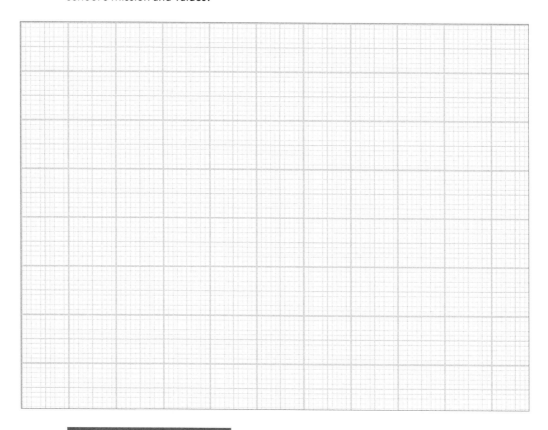

Technology Infrastructure

One of the greatest investments you can make when building a new school or rehabbing an existing one is in technology infrastructure. Technology is as much a part of a digital-age learning environment as are the floors and ceilings. It is now so ubiquitous as to be unnoticeable. "Today's learners want to connect and communicate constantly and want an environment to support these connections (Taylor & Parsons, 2011).

As late as 2014, 70% of public elementary and secondary schools did not have enough broadband access to support widespread use of technology by students (Darling-Hammond, Zielezinski & Goldman, 2014). It is critical for a digital-age school to plan to provide a stable internet connection with sufficient bandwidth; charging stations; technology accessories, such as high-quality microphones, cameras, and 3D printers; and specialized software to facilitate projects in media production, graphic design, and engineering.

A few principles can guide school designers when planning for effective technology integration:

- Include student voices in the design and implementation of technology.
- Provide for long-term storage.
- Support the use of technology to connect students and faculty outside the classroom.
- Embrace the innovation that technology brings, rather just allowing it.
- Use technology to communicate with and engage parents (Nair et al., 2013).

 YOUR TURN

No technology integration process is without its challenges. In your experience, list the major obstacles to successful school-wide technology integration.

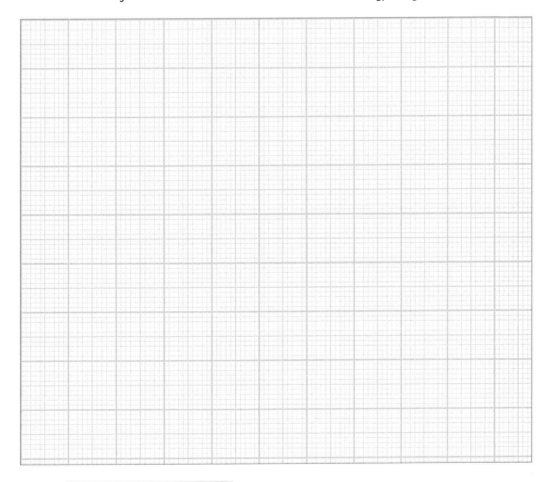

Sustainability

Sustainability is not only "in," it is becoming essential for the health of our planet and ourselves. Related to sustainability is the notion of "high performance," which is a buzzword in school design that refers to the performance of the building itself as well as to those who use it. Sustainable architecture is one feature of high performance design. For schools this translates into a design that:

- Connects to and complements a site's natural features.
- Takes advantage of natural resources from the earth, wind, and sun.
- Uses renewable, recycled, or repurposed materials.
- Manages storm run-off or captures and uses rainwater.
- Takes advantage of natural light.
- Uses healthy paint and carpet materials.

Sustainable design is the perfect avenue for teaching architecture, engineering, construction, and environmental sciences. A project that ties these disciplines together is a school garden project. Participating students can get hands-on work experience while they learn about nutrition, botany, natural resources, geometry, and much more. Another way to engage students in living a healthy and sustainable lifestyle is to encourage active transport options. Doing so can be as straightforward as providing secure, covered bike racks and storage areas that encourage students to bicycle and skateboard to and from school.

Safety and Security

Student safety at school is always a concern for educators and parents, and some may wonder if a learning environment with more open and flexible spaces could invite security breaches or become a breeding ground for student misbehaviors like vandalism and bullying. The term "open" doesn't mean that anyone can come in to a school at any time and do anything they like. Certainly, the usual basic security routines of a school, such as having visitors check in at the office and asking them to wear some kind of identifying badge or nametag, can be incorporated in a school with active learning spaces.

Most schools have designated entry points, often with guards, surveillance cameras, metal detectors, or electronic locks. School designers can look for creative ways to include these features while still maintaining a warm and welcoming environment.

Of course, the best way to discourage bad student behavior is by engaging students in meaningful learning and helping them develop the skills they need to be self-directed and motivated. In an active learning environment, students have more options for personalizing their learning, more input into what and how they learn, and more opportunities for interacting with peers and others. All these characteristics help students to stay involved in constructive, positive learning activities, and so are less likely to look for ways to cause problems.

Still, it would be naive to claim that designing a school with flexible learning spaces will eliminate the need to consider the safety and security of everyone in the building. That said, bullying and harassment often happen in spaces where students are out of the eyes of adults—closed off classrooms, unused nooks and crannies. A safer environment is created when open spaces reduce the barriers that block negative behaviors from view. Thus, a learning environment with flexible spaces should be designed so that students are constantly under the passive supervision of faculty and staff.

Another way of providing a safe school atmosphere is by creating a sense of community among students and staff. Tim Lauer, the principal of Meriwether Lewis Elementary in Portland Oregon, says that in his school the students don't "belong" to an individual teacher: "Everyone, students and teachers alike, has collective responsibility for each other's well being."

> Basically, Transparency and Passive Supervision is the idea of developing a school with high levels of visibility in both formal and informal learning areas. This creates a sense of openness yet preserves acoustic separation, increases natural daylight in the building, and provides the all-important "eyes on the street." (Nair et al., 2013)

 YOUR TURN

Arrange a tour of a local school that has recently been built or redesigned to incorporate active learning spaces. In addition to visiting classrooms, pay attention to the other school spaces both in and outside of the school. Also pay attention to how the school manages to maintain both security and open space.

Beyond the Classroom

If you're lucky enough to be redesigning several spaces within a school, an entire school, or you are building a school from the ground up, then you should consider the other spaces, or potential spaces, available to you. You'll want to discover how these spaces might support your vision and all the people involved in a school.

Imagine a gym that can be divided for large group or small group activities, with doors that lead to an outside area. Envision multi-use equipment that is both team-oriented and individualized that also promotes wellness and health, is fun to use, and gets kids moving. Consider offering activities like yoga, Pilates, juggling, or kickboxing, for example. Now visualize a multipurpose room with a big stage, large screen, projector, and lunch tables. If the lunch tables can be folded and moved to the side when not in use, then the room can also be used for other activities like student performances, presentations, PTA meetings, and other community events.

The Arts

Schools typically departmentalize the arts by offering distinct art classes or even placing the art classrooms in a separate wing of the school. The arts, however are a part of, and not separate from, the other disciplines. Art is ingrained in all subject areas if you take a close look. Technology allows even "non-artists" to make and share their own media creations, for example. In any event, art can be integral to school design. Some ideas for doing so include:

- Have students work with local artists to create art for the school.
- Provide prominent locations for displays of student art and rotate installations frequently.
- Provide places throughout the school that are conducive to impromptu performance.
- Play music on the school PA between classes; use music instead of bells to mark class periods.
- Take advantage of outdoor spaces; perhaps create an outdoor theater or distribute benches for an outdoor classroom.
- Create a soundproof recording studio.

Music is an often-overlooked way of establishing an appropriate mood. Low-level music can be used in a number of ways. Relaxing music can calm students and encourage reflection. Upbeat music can stimulate creativity and enthusiasm. Music, when used artfully, cannot only encourage appropriate emotions in a space, but help to maintain focus during an activity.

But be careful: a Canadian study found conducted in 2004 found that people took up to 20% longer to perform physical and mental tasks to loud music. And if music tempo is above 60 beats per minute, listeners experience a faster heart rate and increased blood pressure, something that would further erode a student's concentration (BBC News, 2004).

Picture all the other spaces for students to grow academically, socially, and emotionally. Hallways can become learning spaces if they feature comfortable chairs, benches, and some tables of varying sizes. The art room can be modified to include a maker lab for students to create things for their projects.

Envision a different library or media center too. By design it may be more open and emptier than current school libraries. It may include small rooms for students to work in, areas for collaboration and team-based work, and spaces for mentoring and tutoring sessions. It may not include desktop computers, but instead may have a device cart with tablets or laptops that students can check out to do research projects, watch video lectures, and catch up on homework. Its collection of books and ebooks may be borrowed using self-checkout systems. QR codes could define sections of the library and highlight student book reviews.

Think about most school bathrooms and locker rooms. Too often these spaces are cramped, dirty, vandalized, poorly maintained, potentially unhygienic, and provide opportunities for bullying. When creating bathrooms in a new school, consider small bathrooms that are distributed throughout the school. Each bathroom should be located next to a supervised area, ideally, and feature stall walls and doors that allow for privacy. Natural light, decorations, and cheerful paint colors can help to make school bathrooms more "homelike."

If the entire school community has a sense that the school is theirs, they will likely take care of it and respect it. Involving students in maintaining and cleaning the school also facilitates a shared sense of ownership. Now, wouldn't that be nice?

YOUR TURN

In the areas provided, write three words you would use to describe your ideal vision for key places within most schools.

Space	Three Words
Gym	
Cafeteria	
Media Center	
Library	
Entryway	
Outdoors	
Art rooms	
Music rooms	
Makerspaces	

Now, use the following workspace to sketch and brainstorm ideal school-wide learning spaces.

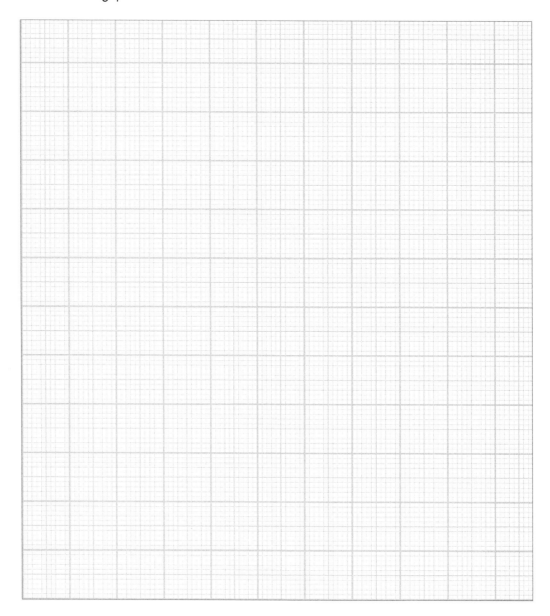

REFLECT & DISCUSS

1. Identify an outside area near a school you know well. How could it be brought into the schools' learning space?
2. Team teaching can facilitate passive supervision of students. How do you feel about team teaching? Is it something you'd support? Why or why not?

Maker Education

Maker education combines problem solving, creativity, and engineering with an ethos of sustainable reuse, playfulness, and social value. Some maker advocates link the maker movement to rediscovering value in shop class and regaining appreciation for tradecraft and technical skills. Other maker advocates focus on its gender-neutral approach to technology-as-craft and its emphasis on production skills in a world that glorifies shopping over creating. Regardless, there are serious pedagogical reasons to pay attention to the maker movement. "Tinkering" epitomizes the "ill-defined" project so valued by constructivists, and of course student-directed and collaborative learning are a big part of the digital-age skill-set. As maker movement founder Dale Dougherty says in his introduction to Curt Gabrielson's book *Tinkering: Kids Learn by Making Stuff*, "Tinkering is a process. It is an attitude. It is the means to fix, make, change, modify, and customize the world (2013)."

The maker movement aligns closely with the principles of active learning spaces. The digital-age demands that learners productively interact with each other and the world around them. Learners who only passively absorb content knowledge from a teacher lecturing from the front of the class run the danger of being left behind. At a time when relatively few people actually understand how our ever more numerous and increasingly complex electronics actually work, students who engage in the practical, real world skills of maker experiences can earn truly valuable knowledge. In addition to these tangible, hands-on skills, the added confidence and advanced thinking skills learned through maker education can help prepare students for their futures, whatever paths they choose to take.

Getting Started with Maker

The maker movement is purposefully broad and undefined. However, one thing is clear: the maker movement is about more than simply making. TechShop CEO and author Mark Hatch identifies Make, Share, Give, Learn, Play, Participate, Support, and Change as the core components of his Maker Manifesto (Hatch, 2013). Few students will be successful makers without the right environment, background knowledge, resources, and community. By creating makerspaces in schools, educators can provide the necessary context for creating student makers. Consider the following ways for teachers to get started:

Craft with Electronics

Maker education makes understanding electronics tangible and fun. A quick search on the internet will identify circuit-building kits designed to provide the foundational skills for students to start creating on their own. University of St. Thomas's Squishy Circuits Project gives students to the necessary knowledge and recipes to explore circuits using basic electronics and conductive and insulating homemade play dough. Students can use playdough to connect components to LEDs, sensors, switches, and more. Chibitronics™

Continued on next page

Continued from previous page

combines crafting with electronics with stick-on LEDs and conductive copper tape. Makey Makey® kits can be used for a wide variety of inventions, and students can use it to program playable bananas and computer games. Students can use kits with a circuit board to turn everyday objects into computer touch-sensors that can activate a computer application. Students can also learn soldering and electronics with a simple kit.

Build with Cardboard and Paper

In makerspaces, cardboard and paper scraps are transformed into building and proto-typing tools that can be used to understand essential concepts of structural engineering. Students apply their geometry skills by measuring, drawing, cutting, and building with cardboard and paper. Websites like Instructables.com provide ready-made plans to get students started building. Once students are inspired and have mastered some basic designs, more than likely they will want to take off with their own designs. They can build a robot, design a bicycle, and more.

Design with an App

The maker movement is closely intertwined with the digital world. Numerous web and tablet applications let students design and construct digitally. Vector drawing apps help users to create drawings that can be sent to a laser cutter for fabrication. Other apps help students create designs for 3D printers. Still other tools give students a chance to test their design ideas for things such as experimental circuits in a virtual environment before prototyping.

Make Space for Makerspaces

Schools around the world are beginning to embrace maker education. Maker education addresses STEAM (Science, Technology, Engineering, Art, Mathematics) standards. Maker education is particularly good for addressing engineering questions where problems are identified and solutions are created. From transforming libraries to building new makerspaces, educators are finding ways to bring maker education into their curricula. Schools with minimal budgets are building their own tables that are suitable for maker projects, while others are purchasing adjustable sturdy tables. Consider carving out a space for maker education in your school. You might be surprised at the ways that teachers and students take advantage of it. Consider the following real-world examples of what other schools are doing.

From Library to Makerspace

Library Media Specialist Leslie Preddy, an award-winning educator from Perry Meridian Middle School in Minneapolis, Minnesota, presented a webinar entitled *Makerspaces: The Now Revolution in School Libraries* (edWeb, 2015). She believes that maker education helps students develop a plethora of skills such as design, collaboration, inquiry, problem solving, invention, and self-direction. She also sees maker education as an opportunity for students to "play." This is because we all learn through play, tinkering, and experimentation—activities that are often downplayed after the early years of school. Maker education is "learning and doing with one's mind," she says. She has been convinced by statements such as: "Students say they have very few opportunities to develop their entrepreneurial energy," and "Nearly half of America's students say they want to start their own business or invent something that changes the world" (Gallup, 2013). Preddy would like to encourage and nurture these aspirations.

Preddy finds motivation in the views of America's youth. In the webinar, she notes the discrepancy between the number of students who want to "start their own business or invent something that changes the world" and the number of opportunities students have to develop their "entrepreneurial energy." Preddy would like to encourage and nurture these aspirations.

To that end, she decided to create "a space like no other in the school." Since the school library is accessible, available to all community members, and open for informal learning after school, it made sense for it to become a makerspace. Preddy was determined to create an intentional space: She wanted people to walk into the space and know they were in a makerspace. Because librarians often see themselves as mentors she had no trouble putting her project into effect. Bookshelves were moved to the peripheral of the space so as to "build a niche into the library." Some shelves were emptied of books and replaced by tools and other maker materials. Old cafeteria tables, donated by the local community center, were set up to offer places for students to engage in "guided makes" with a mentor. All of the furniture pieces are flexible in that they can be easily moved or removed. Preddy is enthusiastic about this new endeavor and draws similarities between gaming and making: "Students can take what they've learned and level up," she explains (2015).

From Shop Room to Innovation Lab

If you attended a traditional public school, you may remember taking an elective shop class. You probably went to a dark classroom that was cluttered with jigsaws, tools, pieces of cut wood, and examples of birdhouses. The floor might have been dusty and the class was mostly comprised of boys because they were generally more drawn to the shop elective than girls. Whatever its qualities, shop class was not essential for academic success for most students. Perhaps it's no surprise that shop class fell out of favor with students, parents, and education leaders.

Shop is making a comeback in the form of makerspaces. The Ann Richards School for Young Women Leaders in Austin, Texas, had two shop classrooms that were collecting dust. Teacher Kat Sauter was convinced that maker education would benefit her girls. She

Continued on next page

Continued from previous page

shared her work in the webinar *Intel Teach Live: How Do We Empower and Inspire Young Women?* (Intel® Education, 2015).

Sauter had a vision and with the help of parents, students, and community members, that vision was realized. The shop classrooms were transformed into "innovation labs." Some windows were removed and a garage door was installed to allow for natural light and fresh air. The space now opens to another space—the outdoors—where students can also work. Since the two rooms were becoming makerspaces, the doors were removed and windows were installed between the classrooms. The wood from the doors was repurposed and used to build the tables.

The lab has round tables, comfortable chairs, 3D printers, and laser engravers. Other fun stuff includes littleBits™ kits, Raspberry Pi™ boards, Makey Makey® kits, and Tinker cards. Laptops have Autodesk® 3D modeling software on them. The school participates in Project Lead the Way, which focuses on engineering and STEAM. Sauter believes that through maker education and design thinking, students learn important life, learning, and 21st-century skills.

 **CASE STUDY**

A Digital-Age School
Design39Campus: A New Way and Place to Learn

At Design39Campus (D39C) students have "superpowers," learn in "Studios, Makeries, and Collaboratories" with "Learning Experience Designers" (LEDs), exercise in the "Fitness Center," and lunch at the "Food Court." *It's a college, right?* No! It's a public school in Poway Unified District near San Diego, California. The school opened its doors to prekindergarten (PK) through sixth grade in August of 2014 and will eventually grow to include middle school and a total of 1,400 lucky students. The student population, which is ethnically and economically diverse, has the opportunity to experience a brand new campus and a different approach to learning.

Getting Ready

In 2012, the superintendent of Poway Unified tasked the entire district with "changing the way we do schools," explains Megan Power, a Learning Experience Designer (LED) and one of the designers of Design39Campus. To support this effort, the district removed a principal from one school, and for two years challenged her to research and plan a brand new school. In the second planning year, five teachers were brought in to help design and provide practical insights and expertise. Their charge was to discover how to provide a different and better learning environment for students! Using Design Thinking, they worked through the same processes that they would be expecting their students to use throughout their learning experiences.

Figure 5.1: Design39Campus in Poway, CA

Empathize: During the Empathy stage, the design team researched different schools through virtual and face-to-face visitations of schools and businesses. They traveled to the d.school at the Stanford University Institute of Design, took d.school MOOCs (Massive Open Online Courses) on designing new learning environments, watched relevant Ted Talks, and read books.

The team conducted focus groups with community members to imagine what the school should be like and the opportunities they would like students to have. Interviewees used the following sentence stems to visualize the not-yet-built school:

- Students could...
- Teachers who...
- Principals who...
- Parents who...

Define: The design team explored three questions to document current educational practices that they were using and identify problems:

- Why is it that we're doing it this way?
- Why is it typically done this way?
- Is there a better way?

"We looked at anything you could imagine about schools, and asked ourselves: Is it something we need or is it something we don't need anymore? Is it something that needs changing? If so, what do we need to change about it?" says Power. "We had deep conversations about everything, including the types of furniture conducive to our vision, the spaces we wanted, how the spaces would be used, how students would learn, and the structure of leadership."

Ideate: During the ideation stage, the group worked with parents, community members, and businesses to collect ideas for the new school. They also did a two-week project with fourth and fifth graders using Design Thinking to brainstorm answers to questions such as: What are different ways we can do certain things? How can we restructure a classroom, and a school? "We were pleasantly surprised to hear that some of the students' ideas were similar to ours and knew we were on the right track," expresses Power.

Prototyping and Testing: The team worked closely with the BakerNowicki architects and a school furniture company to put their ideas into a plan and start building. "We are still prototyping and testing our ideas, constantly reevaluating and changing things," says Power. "We think of ourselves as a startup company, and we will always be a startup company. It's all about changing, getting back to that empathy piece and research piece, prototyping, and asking ourselves, Is it working? What do we need to change and adapt?" The designers look to their students and ask them for help because they're the experts—it's their learning and education.

Figure 5.2: D39C Welcomes the community

A Campus Tour

Driving up to D39C, one can't help but be impressed by the colored-glass edifice with a student-designed garden in front. A fully retractable front gate opens to the school, where a windowed "Welcome Center" invites visitors and students into the "campus" and establishes the tone of transparency, community, and the importance of space.

The campus includes four buildings: The Showcase, The Welcome Center, and two classroom buildings. The principal, office staff, and "Welness Center" staff share a design studio space in the Welcome Center. Sitting on a small hill across from the Welcome Center is the Showcase building, which houses a multipurpose space, cafeteria, and music room. Across from the Showcase are two 2-storey classroom buildings at different elevations, with a common promenade between them and three bridges connecting them. Each building has "pods" or multi-grade clusters of learning spaces.

The Welcome Center

The Principal, Vice-Principal and administrative staff share an open space, atypical of the more common school offices. The idea behind a shared space mirrors the rest of the school design and philosophy; spaces that are accessible to all, flexible, collaborative, and communal. Not to mention that office equipment and supplies are more readily accessible. The health center is also housed in the Welcome Center.

Figure 5.3: The Showcase, a multi-purpose room

The Showcase Building

Outside, the single-level Showcase building is flanked by outdoor tables, a covered pavilion for basketball and volleyball, and a landscaped tiered lawn. Beneath the Showcase is an expansive open green space, with play structures, a track, open fields, and pickle-ball courts. Inside is the "Showcase" (a multipurpose room), the "Servery" (a school food court), the "Fitness Center" (gym), and a sound-proofed music room. The names of the spaces, embossed on metal placards, send a strong message that this is no ordinary school.

The Showcase Room

Central to the Showcase building is the Showcase itself, a multipurpose room. In seconds, the room can be transformed to an indoor lunch space, an open space for whole school gatherings, an auditorium for performances, a presentation hall, and meeting room for large meetings. The room is a flexible space with modular furniture that changes throughout the day depending on its use. Tables can be joined together for picnic benches, pulled apart for watching presentation, and transformed into stadium seating benches in a matter of minutes. The renewable wooden-ceilinged room is naturally lit by the three glass garage doors that open.

The Fitness Studio

The indoor Fitness Studio, aside the Showcase space, separates into three rooms when the room divider is used. Multipurpose equipment fills the room and garage doors open to the outdoor fitness area called the Pavilion. This space has a rubberized floor, holes in the ground for nets, and a roof for sun or rain protection. A redesigned Physical Education program called Minds in Motion happens here. All students participate and exercise with offerings such as yoga, hula hooping, collaborative games, and dancing, to name just a few.

Figure 5.4: The Fitness Studio, a place for Minds in Motion

The Servery and Food Court

The Servery dishes out the typical school lunch, while in the other room, the Food court offers a menu-of-the-day with a variety of choices, such as Mexican, American, and Italian, and is broadcasted on a flat screen TV. Not only do students have more choices but the choices are healthier than those typically found in a school. Outdoor tables are scattered outside the Servery. Students, however, are allowed to eat anywhere until music calls them in from lunch. That's right—music instead of bells sends the students dancing to class!

The Music Studio

A music and band room, down a hall from the Showcase room provides a space for singing and playing instruments, of course. But it is also a place used for musical theater or Minds in Motion dance. The room has soundproofing panels and an audio recording studio is planned for the future.

Staff and Parent Spaces

Parents and community members are invited to use the spaces on campus. A staff lunchroom in the Welcom Center, called Café 39, has small tables and decorations. The planning team took the time to visit businesses known for their architectural designs. "We heard them talk about their eating spaces and how important it is for relationship building, and not work," Power says with excitement. "We didn't want it to look like a typical staff room," she adds. "To that end, all parents, volunteers, and staff are welcome to a similar lunch with an open door, where no work is done and students are not discussed."

Figure 5.5: Cafe 39, an eatery for staff

A staff workroom exists but doesn't see much use. Yes, they have a copy machine, but since the school is BYOD and uses digital books, the copy machine isn't heavily used, which saves on paper and expensive maintenance and repair costs. Glass-walled rooms near the workroom provide spaces for parents and staff to meet. A parent hall area offers movable whiteboard panels, supplies such as letterhead, envelopes, and Post-Its®. D39C welcomes parents in any way they can be involved in the school.

Classroom Buildings

Across from the Showcase Building sit a paired set of two-storied classroom buildings that sit face-to-face at slightly different elevations with connecting bridges. The Promenade is an open space between the two buildings, with chalkboard walls, outdoor work spaces, and planters. Classroom doors lead out to the promenade and the chalkboard-covered walls.

Figure 5.6: Promenade view of classroom buildings

Pods

Each of the buildings is for "Pods". Pods are multi-grade groups within the school that share common spaces, teachers, and resources. "Currently we have six pods: two Transitional Kindergarten, Kindergarten, and 1st Grade pods, two second and third grade pods, and two fourth, fifth, and sixth grade pods." Pods include five to six Learning Experience Designers (LEDs), including a resource LED. LEDs and students move around in the Pod, depending on what they are doing," explains Powers.

Unlike most schools, teachers at D39C, don't have their own classrooms. But they do have their own homerooms so that they can connect with a set group of students. Each Pod includes classrooms, or Learning Studios, one of which is a double classroom with a wall that can close or open easily.

Learning Studios

Entering one of the Learning Studios, you see a wide open space, with furniture that can easily slide out of the way when students are doing something that requires a lot of space. Within a few seconds, students can pull the wheeled whiteboard-topped tables out and set up the room for any kind of learning experience.

Personal belongings are stored in restaurant-style bus tub bins (they are the perfect size for backpacks and lunch boxes). Parents are told not to provide their children with larger rolling bags because students do not lug around textbooks. The shelves were built to hold the bus tubs and also double as standing workplaces.

Figure 5.7: A Learning Studio with mobile furniture and carts with bins along the wall

Within each Studio, whiteboards line several walls. Each of these walls can be used for projection, and students can easily note or sketch their work on a whiteboard. With multiple whiteboard walls, the "front" of the room goes away. A rolling cart holds a projector and supplies, and it can be easily moved anywhere. Whiteboard-topped tables are mobile and multi-use. Recently, a balloon experiment failed outside on a windy day, so students went back inside and reset the room to an open space for the experiment. "This would never have happened in a traditional room; there would have been tables, desks, and chairs in the way. Space can change to what we need it for in an instant," explains Power.

The Makery

Every Pod has a Makery, or maker space, for deconstructing and constructing electronics, repurposing vacuums and computers, building catapults, exploring mechanical engineering, being artistic, and making a mess, for example. Many learning experiences incorporate making. The high, industrial-strength and stationary Makery tables have stools that slide all the way underneath. Neatly organized movable storage bins on shelves line the back wall.

Figure 5.8: A Makery, a space for tinkering

The Collaboratory

Large Collaboratories are open spaces for each Pod that look more like lounges than typical public school spaces. Each floor has three Collaboratories. Collaboratories offer space for just about anything, collaboration, individual work, and presentations. Each Callaboratory is carpeted and has soft furniture, movable tables and chairs, Hokki stools of different sizes, whiteboards, cameras, and charging stations. The youngest Pod has an Imagination Station in addition to a Collaboratory, another open space where students can play, discover, or engage in simulations, such as transforming the space into a store to develop math skills.

Figure 5.9: A Collaboratory, a space for individual, small and large group work

The Loft

The Loft, aka library, is in one of the classroom buildings, open on one side as a loft. Like all other roms, it too is a flexible space that welcomes large groups, small groups, and is open during lunch. Small and large meeting rooms allow for different activities to go on at the same time. Books are checked out on the honor system. Within the Loft is a computer lab, but it doesn't have computers because this is a BYOD (Bring Your Own Device) school and devices are used all around the campus.

The Gallery

The Gallery lies below the loft, connected by an open staircase and is a campus-wide common space where students usually give Ted Talk–style presentations. It has tiered, built-in seating and three flat screen monitors on the walls for students to project their work. One of the screens can even be split into four screens!

Pod Learning

A different kind of school building and student organization requires a different kind of teacher and student planning and learning. To make the Pod structure work, teachers within a Pod have a one-hour meeting every morning in the a "Design Studio", a meeting room devoted to the LEDs of each Pod. Here, they plan what they're going to do, determine what they are going to offer students, discuss how students are doing; and decide if they need to regroup in different ways. They plan long-term learning experiences, similar to projects. They also discuss "Deep Dives," which are similar to electives, except that the area of study is entirely based on the interests of the students.

The curriculum at D39C is designed around a continuum of ideas and skills through which students progress at their own rate. Collaboration, creativity, and critical thinking are emphasized in all subject areas. The curricular pathways provide a comprehensive and cohesive experience that builds upon fluencies and skills for each student as he or she progresses. Integration of subject matters is a key ingredient to help students make connections in their learning.

As for the Common Core State Standards, "We believe that Common Core is the floor, the jumping off point. It's where we start at and then we jump off from there," Power says. Design39 teachers are able to develop and design their own curriculum by working with students and with each other. They use digital textbooks and other resources. "We want to be able to practice the art of teaching, where we're working with students and each other to create learning experiences," adds Power. "Since everyone has superpowers, teachers and students can capitalize on those during learning experiences. At Design39, we're about growth mindset, not fixed mindset—it's not about getting the grade, it's about growing. We want to show growth and progress in each of our students."

Design39Campus opened in August 2014 as a brand-new school. As the last and 39th school in Poway Unified School District, the school is based on Design Thinking for learning experiences within active learning spaces, and all of the spaces reflect that mission.

Student population: More than 800 (2015); 1,400 in 2017 (proposed)

Enrollment: Optional enrollment, through a lottery, for participating Mello-Roos districts within the Poway Unified School District

Construction funding: Community Facilities Districts special taxes

Architect: BakerNowicki

Who's In Charge?

"In reimagining a school, we wanted to change everything, especially how we named the people and spaces within a school so that everyone would know that this is a different kind of school," explains Power, "Naming teachers as Learning Experience Designers defies the image that people have of who teachers are and what they do. At our campus, everyone is a teacher!" In fact, students are also LEDs because they, too, are learning to design their experiences. As students and teachers learn together at Design39, each person is recognized with their own "superpower," meaning special skills that they can share with others to create learning experiences. Superpowers can be skills such as filming, video editing, reading aloud, writing poetry, performing, or mentoring. The intent is to break down the roles of teacher and student; to flatten the hierarchy and elevate the student's role.

"We believe in flat leadership. We do have a principal and vice principal, but they're not the decision-makers on campus. We all have the power to make decisions. For Pod decisions, whatever we need or changes we want to make, we don't have to ask permission. We have that trust," explains Power. "When decisions are made, they're made by those people who have superpowers, or who are passionate in those areas. Ideally, the principal will be more like a CEO of the school who is making connections, helping Design39 to connect with businesses, gets funding, and who does 'a ton of design thinking.'"

ISTE Essential Condition: Empowered Leaders

"Stakeholders at every level empowered to be leaders in effecting consistent system-wide change."

While leadership can be assumed to come from administrators, a shift to a more cooperative model of decision making capitalizes on individual strengths and expertise and creates a more invested community. The elevated role of teachers in decision making at Design39 exemplifies this critical element of both successful technology integrations and school design projects.

What the Future Holds

The architects of Design39 designed a campus with open possibilities and are proud to see the spaces that they have established haven't reverted back to a traditional way of schooling. Keep an eye on Design39 to follow along with their dreams. Megan Power and others in the school have an ambitious goal— they want to change education for students all over the world! They welcome visitors to see the campus and to talk with the staff and students. By sharing what's happening at D39C, they want to continue to grow, learn, and change how students learn, and the spaces in which they learn, in communities all over the globe. Learn more about Design39Campus at https://sites.google.com/site/design39campus/.

CHAPTER

6

Digital Spaces for Learning

By David Jakes, ed tech leader and blogger

The space where learning occurs is sometimes referred to as the "third teacher," along with the influences of adults and peers (Cannon Design, 2011). Undoubtedly, how learners engage with each other, with ideas, and with the resources associated with learning is shaped and influenced by the environment in which those interactions occur.

The emergence and availability of digital tools and the environments that employ the connective and creative potential of technology are fundamentally reshaping what constitutes an educational experience, as well as where it occurs, and what it means to be well-educated. Concepts such as "Digital-age learning" and "next generation learning spaces" represent a potential ecology of skills, habits, and dispositions that are acquired through a variety of interactions shaped by new types of learning environments, including dedicated digital spaces for learning.

Many schools are now providing digital tools for learning through 1:1 technology programs or by leveraging the capacity of student-owned technology to support learning. This increased access to technology for students is a disruptive influence on the status quo of education, and is directly challenging what learning can look like in schools. Given that, it is essential that schools begin widening the conversation around technology to incorporate a discussion of the creation of digital spaces for learning. These spaces can create a more expansive condition for where and how learning can occur and start a dialogue regarding what schools want to accomplish educationally beyond simply acquiring devices. What these devices connect to—and how they serve learning—should be fundamental questions that all schools address.

The opportunity to create a larger landscape for learning that supports new and engaging learning experiences is a compelling proposition. The combination of physical and digital learning spaces has the opportunity to create a new ecology for learning, one that focuses on the needs of today's learners and is designed to support the development of a learning community across a wide range of interactions and spaces (Hilton, 2013).

Exploring the creation of digital learning spaces for learning involves a thoughtful consideration of the questions that inform the process of establishing, implementing, using, and evaluating such spaces. Specifically, these questions are:

- Is the concept of "classroom" defined only by a physical space still relevant?
- How do the expectations for a student learning experience shape the development of an ecology of learning spaces?
- What are the characteristics of a digital space that is part of this ecology?
- What constitutes a "next generation" ecology of learning spaces?
- What are the potential shifts in the educational experience that occur by realizing a more expansive condition of space where learning can occur?

 **YOUR TURN**

Choose one or more of the above questions to answer in the space below and begin exploring the creation of digital learning spaces.

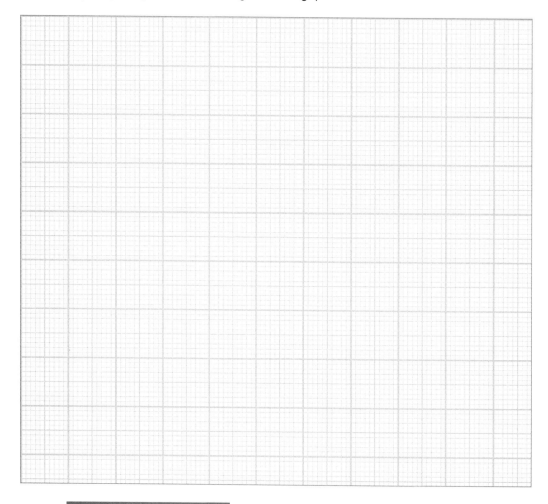

The Concept of "Classroom"

While the classroom may have been considered the primary location of learning in schools, the same spaces that have served learners for decades are in need of rethinking in this age of technology and global connectedness. Traditional classroom designs limit opportunities to reshape the space to support the range of learning interactions required to develop the dispositions that favor success in a networked world in perpetual "beta." Accomplishing this means discarding the traditional notion of what a "classroom" is. Such a mindset promotes the conditions necessary for the development of a new type of contemporary learning space, one no longer constrained by the historical configuration of the schoolhouse classroom.

Beyond rethinking and reshaping the physical space to become more flexible, agile, and adaptive, ubiquitous technology creates an opportunity to add a new dimension to the concept of where and how students learn. Because of this technology, the addition of a digital space for learning can transform the "classroom" into a broader concept, one that presents expansive and boundless conditions for learning. Creating these conditions moves the construct of classroom from an isolated relic of the past into a space that merges a centering location for learning (physical space) with a digital space that is always on, accessible 24-7 from a variety of devices, and supports connective and networked interactions that create new opportunities for learning that extend beyond the brick and mortar school.

The Student Learning Experience as Design Driver

Learning spaces, whether they are physical or digital, should be designed to support the learning experience for students. Too often spaces are created by focusing on "things" (furniture, interactive whiteboards, and so forth) and not on the expectations for what students will do as learners (collaborate, create). Schools should begin with learning behaviors, and build learning spaces that have the capacity to support the development of these behaviors. Doing this requires focusing on the skills and habits that students need to learn, the dispositions that they need to exhibit, and how they will demonstrate and make visible their understanding. It is also critical to consider how spaces will support student agency and choice, and how they will support participation and contribution. The addition of digital spaces for learning provides an additional context for the learning experience, and requires the same consideration of how they will be constructed to support *and extend* the student learning experience.

Characteristics of a Digital Learning Space

With the variety of tools that are available to schools, what are the characteristics of a comprehensive digital space? In answering this question, schools should consider creating a digital ecology that features spaces that they themselves create and provide (just like formal physical classrooms), while honoring student agency in shaping their digital experience with the tools that they choose to employ. Consider the types of spaces where learning occurs and how they can be adapted to support digital-age learning.

School-Owned Spaces

Schools have the opportunity to create digital spaces for teachers and students. These spaces, along with the physical classrooms of the school, create *a foundation* for building a learning environment that is scalable and that provides systemic and guaranteed tools for digital learning. These are:

- Spaces for Educators: create spaces that enable educators to have an online presence that provides students with 24-7 access to the resources and school connections that they need to be successful. These spaces should support communication, curation, discussion forums, chats, online assessments, and enable third party apps, tools, and resources to be added to increase functionality and capacity.
- Spaces for Students: students should have access to a digital space that supports a wide range of interactions and capabilities, and that is reconfigurable and adaptable. Students should have choice on how they use this space. That is, they should have a sense of ownership even though the school provides the space. Such a space should provide a unique personal space for digital learning as well as an interface for collaboration and creation.

Student-Owned Spaces

Schools must realize that their students have used technology, in some capacity, for the majority of their lives. Recognizing that they use online tools to self-organize their needs for learning is essential. For example, tools such as Twitter and Facebook (as well as many others) provide a social platform for learning that should be accepted and embraced. If necessary, and as age appropriate, these tools should be available during the school day. These types of spaces add depth and dimension to the spaces owned by schools, and the inclusion and acceptance of such spaces creates a layer of choice for students that empowers engagement and recognizes the social and personal nature of learning.

Design Considerations

There are three key design considerations for the types of digital spaces that support learning. These are:

- Mobile: Digital learning spaces should be accessible anywhere and at anytime across a range of device types.
- Responsive design: Digital learning spaces should provide a universal experience across the different devices that students may use (desktop, laptop, tablet, and smartphone). This is especially true in schools that focus their efforts on a BYOT (Bring Your Own Technology) environment where students have a variety of devices.
- Personalized: Digital learning spaces should be designed to offer a range of services, tools, and capacities that can be chosen by the user to create an individual experience. Spaces should be designed as a "canvas" or "palette" that supports choice and enables students to self-select the tools that they will use, while allowing them to add their own tools.

> ## ISTE Essential Condition: Equitable Access
>
> "All students, teachers, staff and school leaders have robust and reliable connectivity and access to current and emerging technologies and digital resources."
>
> Modern learning spaces need to provide equitable access to technological devices to support digital learning for all students, including those traditionally underserved or with special needs. This includes not only appropriate numbers of devices and levels of connectivity but also teachers who understand how to leverage technology for the most disadvantaged students.

Tools for Digital Space Creation

New tools that support the creation of digital learning spaces are emerging each day. It is a landscape that features traditional tools such as learning management systems that support teaching and learning, to course platforms that provide students with a fully integrated course experience. Massive open online courses (MOOCs) may have thousands enrolled, and they create educational experiences that are connected and distributed across the networks of the internet.

Given the availability and capacity of digital tools, how these tools are specifically employed to create a digital learning space platform is dependent upon the school's organizational readiness for change, its capacity to support and maintain technology, the cost of the tools, and the school's vision of the desired student learning experience.

Learning Management Systems

Employing a learning management system, such as Canvas, Haiku, Blackboard, Moodle, or Edmodo, is an approach that many learning institutions follow. These tools are scalable, or generally easy to use. As well, they deliver a consistent landscape for educators and students, and provide interoperability across devices. Many of these platforms now allow for the integration of third-party elements that extend the platform's capability to support learning. Such a tool provides an acceptable solution for creating the digital spaces for educators, as described earlier. Other similar platforms include Edmodo, Pearson's Open-Class, and Google Classroom.

Tool Suites

Tools such as Google Apps for Education and Microsoft's Office 365 provide a comprehensive suite of tools that enable schools to create flexible and agile spaces for students. For example, Google Apps provides access to Google Drive with its apps and storage capacity, Hangouts (the Google Plus social platform),YouTube, Sites, Blogger, Gmail, and Calendar. Additionally, Google Apps provides seamless integration with Chromebooks, Google Play Tablets, and Google Classroom. Office 365 provides online access to widely recognized software that includes Microsoft Word, PowerPoint, and Excel. Both platforms provide students with communication and content-creation tools that give them the flexibility to engage as digital learners in a variety of capacities.

Apps Ecosystems

A wide variety of applications that are readily accessible across platforms are available to learners today. Apps that are available on smartphones and tablets enable students to create additional capacity for learning. Online software such as WeVideo (video creation) and Evernote (content curation) are examples of software hosted in "the cloud." Even internet browsers, such as Google Drive, can host applications and browser extensions that support learning.

Social Media

Simply put, social media tools connect people. Tools such as Twitter, Facebook, Instagram, and YouTube, among others, provide schools with the capacity to connect with stakeholders and learners through a variety of media interfaces. These types of tools have become embedded in our culture, and they must be considered as an element of any digital learning space. How these are leveraged specifically to support and enhance learning still needs to be addressed more fully, but there is no doubt that these tools can be used to effectively distribute content and ideas.

There are very few limits to the digital learning space that can't be overcome with today's technology tools. Because of the flexibility and enormous number of tools, digital learning spaces are inherently agile and can be configured in different arrangements, either by the student, the school, or by both.

YOUR TURN

Think about different categories of digital tools. Use the following table to document how you are currently using digital tools to create digital spaces for learning in your classroom, school, or district. Then, spend time brainstorming additional uses for these tools.

Tools for Digital Space Creation	Current Uses	Potential Uses
Learning Management Systems		
Tool Suites		
Apps Ecosystems		
Social Media		

Toward a Next Generation Ecology of Spaces

The combination of physical and digital space represents a larger ecology of space for learning. These spaces are linked together and support the learning experience equally because learning in one space informs learning in the other. The two spaces, considered together, can be said to form *a multidimensional learning space* (Bretag, 2011).

A multidimensional space supports academic activities in both physical and digital domains ranging from individual learning experiences to collaborative opportunities. Because of this, it is important to consider that the skills (such as collaboration) and habits (such as thinking interdependently) of learners must be developed in two types of learning conditions. For example, it is reasonable to expect all students to master collaboration skills, but in today's reality that means learning how to collaborate face-to-face as well as online. It also means learning how to collaborate synchronously in real time with peers as well as asynchronously as a "give and take" experience. A multidimensional space provides schools with the environment to help students develop this skill duality and helps support the development of dispositions that serve students in either type of learning space.

Spatial Insights

To explore the spatial implications of technology-empowered learning, the Steelcase Education team completed a design research study in 2014 that involved 16 schools, colleges, and universities throughout the United States. The team also interviewed educators, administrators, technologists, and students at the primary, secondary, and higher education levels.

One of the study's "Six Spatial Insights" was that learning spaces must be designed to both capture and stream information. These spaces must support audio and lighting needs for creating video content (Steelcase Education, 2014).

Instructors' offices are being adapted to become "recording studios" for creating online content, and webcams are being added to classrooms to capture class activities. Educators are increasingly using videoconferencing to connect with subject matter experts around the world while students use the technology for team assignments and study groups. Teachers are even employing video as an evaluation tool for student-presented content or to demonstrate practical skills. By videorecording presentations of practical skills, students can assess their own performance in addition to getting feedback from peers and the teacher.

Investments in both space and appropriate technology can ensure an optimum learning environment regardless of the physical location of educator or students.

Schools should also consider adding a digital knowledge commons to the multidimensional space for exchanging and accessing collectively owned information and content. This space allows members of the school community to share their expertise and passions around learning. A digital knowledge commons allows students to add their expertise to a community pool of knowledge and connect with other individuals with similar interests. The addition of this type of space adds an informal and more social context for learning, and develops connections among learners that might not otherwise occur. Such a space breaks down barriers and engages individuals and groups across the typical boundaries associated with schools.

The Impact of Active Digital-Age Learning Spaces

Creating new *conditions* for learning can begin by creating new *spaces* for learning. Establishing a digital learning space and linking it intentionally with the physical spaces of schools can promote a variety of shifts in the educational experience of school. These can include:

1. **A shift in the school's ability to prepare students for an increasingly digital life.** Successfully negotiating the digital spaces that are available to students today requires guidance and support from more experienced users. Creating digital school spaces for students provides a location for learners where they can be mentored and grow as digital learners in preparation for a more connected learning experience.

2. **A shift from an isolated to a connected experience.** Adding digital school spaces provides an interface between the school and larger digital world, and increases learners' capacity to network and receive a more enriched experience. Such a shift recognizes that schools today are a single node in a distributed ecology of spaces where students can learn, and that these additional locations add value to the educational lives of students by connecting them to ideas, resources, conversations, and other learners.

3. **A shift in how, when, and where learning occurs.** Digital spaces enable schools to add additional types of learning experiences, including blended or online courses that they develop. Adding these types of courses requires that schools rethink where students learn, how school days could potentially be restructured, and how physical spaces can be re-created to support a more digital learning experience. This also includes developing new pedagogies that specifically leverage the affordances of digital technologies (Sköld, 2012).

4. **A shift in the resources available to learners and educators.** There is an enormous repository of resources online that are available for learning, often available for no charge. These range from a variety of media that supports learning (imagery, audio, video, simulations, and animations), to open educational resources (OER), to freely available courses from major universities. Having digital spaces for learning enables schools to assemble these resources in purposeful ways and connect their learners to unique digital opportunities for learning (Vander Ark, 2015).

5. **A shift in the ability of the school to be innovative.** The overlap between physical and digital spaces, as well as between school and the world, creates an "edge" experience. These spaces, where communities overlap, provide more diverse conditions for the emergence and development of innovative thoughts, conversations, and ideas that can transform learning. Innovative institutions seek to create edges as a technique that can fuel innovation (Hagel, Brown & Davison, 2010).

6. **A shift in how students interact with their world.** Digital learning environments impact how students participate and contribute as a learner. Students can create and publish to either a school or worldwide audience with a click or a tap. Such spaces grant students agency to act on their own as a learner, and give them a choice in how they participate in a learning path that can be individualized so as to create a personal learning experience.

The addition of digital learning spaces increases the capacity of schools to engage their learners in meaningful and compelling experiences. These spaces support an enhanced richness of experience, permitting students to make choices in how, when, why, and where they learn, as well as who they learn with.

The essence of learning in these spaces is that they empower learners to network, process information, repurpose it, and create and share, while having their ideas challenged by other learners, without the limitations of place, space, and time.

 REFLECT & DISCUSS

1. What is the relationship between the physical classroom and digital space in active learning?
2. How can you, your school, or your district leverage social media for learning and telling your school's story?
3. In your opinion, why is the establishment of digital learning spaces essential for the digital age?

CASE STUDY

Plymouth Rocks Learning Spaces
Inside Indiana's Weidner School of Inquiry

Figure 6.1: An open classroom featuring flexible furniture solutions to promote collaboration and group study

The Weidner School of Inquiry in Plymouth, Indiana, is more than just a school: It's a school *inside* of a school. Located inside of Plymouth High School (which has a student body of approximately 1,200), the Weidner School of Inquiry is an ambitious and highly successful project-based program—not a charter school—that gives its students a hand-on approach to learning. It is an alternative learning environment that allows students to explore and make connections with the world around them.

The school was founded in 2012 and occupies a brand new space that was formerly a second floor swimming pool. The Weidner School of Inquiry is a small learning environment with its own staff and administration. It was started as a choice for Plymouth High School students who wanted to experience project-based learning. The students take approximately half to two-thirds of their total coursework each year in the Weidner's learning environment, utilizing project-based learning as the instructional pedagogy.

As part of the New Tech Network (NTN)—a nonprofit organization that takes a project-based learning approach to engaging students with dynamic, rigorous curriculum—the school's mission is to prepare students not only for college but also for life beyond the classroom. It does so by utilizing the 4Cs—Creativity,

Collaboration, Communication, and Critical Thinking—to build a foundation of skills that will support students as they enter the working world. This approach—according to Jennifer Felke, co-director at Weidner School of Inquiry—is a direct response to the traditional school model (based on the transfer and memorization of specific learning content from teacher to student), which she feels doesn't adequately prepare students for adult life.

Figure 6.2: A classroom featuring hanging writeboards to present the work of students and groups to the entire class

"The days of the 'sage on the stage' are numbered," Felke says. "We need to continue to do a better job of emphasizing 21st-century skill development in addition to providing engaging survey courses that spark passions and potential career path exploration; cultivating the skill-sets students will need for 21st-century jobs. Especially at the high school-level, we need to reimagine what the learning process is all about."

A huge part of this "reimagining" effort centers on the physical space in which this new style of learning is set. Logically, in the school's quest to develop digital-age skills, the school itself mimics, in many ways, a modern workplace.

The renovated facility houses six double classrooms meant to accommodate 50 students each, along with three single classrooms and three small technology-infused collaboration rooms. All classrooms have projectors and screens, with double classrooms having between three to five screens in the room and a microphone system. The school's large "Navy Room" has a large center screen in addition to four corner screens for projection, and also features a bleacher seating area that can easily accommodate 100 people.

The first floor has three distinct flex spaces with two more flex zones on the second floor of the open loft-style main commons. These spaces are filled with comfortable, moveable furniture that encourages active learning and promotes easy collaboration on student-led projects. The classrooms themselves are furnished with tables that seat eight students. There is no formal front of the classroom, which ensures that, during whole group instruction, no student has a bad seat, and that there is always the opportunity for full-engagement.

Additionally, these spaces act as practice areas for formalized clubs such as BPA (Business Professionals of America) and speech class. In addition, the school boasts a makerspace that promotes hands-on learning. It is used mainly by science courses for classes like Bio-Art, Chem-Food Science, and Physics-Sustainable Energy. All rooms utilize a "room wizard," which is an electronic scheduler that is located outside each door. There is also a courtyard area outside of the school's first floor annex where a community garden or an outside collaboration area may soon be developed.

"The aesthetics of a learning space impacts our students from the moment they walk into a facility," explains Weidner School of Inquiry co-director Michael Delp. "Is the space open and inviting? Does it encourage collaboration and connection? Is the design and color engaging to those working in the space? Does it promote openness and opportunities to be creative? These are the questions we must ask ourselves when thinking about learning spaces. And we have seen firsthand that active learning spaces can promote student engagement."

Success by Design

Figure 6.3: The first-floor of the Weidner School of Inquiry features flexible areas for study and collaboration. ©Susan Fleck Photography, 2013

In May of 2014, the Weidner School of Inquiry was named New Tech Network's first Demonstration Site for the 2014–15 school year. This distinction was due to the school's emerging structures and practices that align with the NTN Learning

Organization Framework; its instructional alignment with college and career readiness; its sustained instructional quality; and its cultural alignment with college and career readiness.

In addition, Weidner was named a P21 Exemplary School—one of only 15 in the country—in December of that same year. During a site visit, P21 evaluated the school on the following indicators:

- Evidence of commitment to college, career, and life readiness
- Educational support systems and sustainable design
- Engaged learning approaches
- Equitable student access to digital-age learning
- Evidence of student acquisition of digital-age knowledge and skills
- Partnerships for sustainable success

The Weidner School of Inquiry At a Glance

- Codirectors: Michael Delp and Jennifer Felke
- Start Year: 2012
- Grade levels: 9–12
- Number of students: Approximately 300 (will cap at 400)
- Staff: Seventeen
- Location: Plymouth High School, Plymouth, Indiana

Felke notes that the school's success is due, in part, to the space's encouragement of movement while accommodating different groupings of students from pairs to multi-student teams. This movement and engagement affects how students interact with one another. It also affects how they work with their facilitators and any community member or subject matter expert who happens to participate in a given learning session.

Weidner collaborated with the Fort Wayne, Indiana, architectural firm Barton-Coe-Vilamaa on the school's design, with the staff traveling to Steelcase, Inc. in Grand Rapids, Michigan, to learn more about how the design and components of a learning environment can affect students. The superintendent and staff later researched best practices to establish a learning space that would facilitate the development of digital-age skills with a focus on creativity, collaboration, and communication. The school wrote several grants and partnered with community businesses to support a fundraising effort that reached nearly $750,000. In the fall of 2014, Barton-Coe-Vilamaa won an AIA Design Award for their work on the Weidner School of Inquiry.

Felke and Delp assumed the oversight of the school in 2014. Both had previously served as teachers during the school's first year. The first year of the program was led by Kenneth Olson as the sole director. Olson has since returned to his former position as dean of students at Plymouth High School. Felke previously taught at Oregon-Davis Junior/Senior High School; while Delp served as Plymouth High

School's tennis, basketball, and golf coach and also led several initiatives, including Flipped Instruction.

In their co-director roles—the only co-leadership team in the New Tech Network—Felke and Delp have the unique opportunity to fulfill the school's mission to help students identify and pursue their passions in a positive culture and engaging environment through project-based learning. They understand that physical spaces are critical to the project-based curriculum and help to set the tone for learning. "The professional appearance of the space, combined with frequent involvement from community professionals, has played a transformative role in helping our learners change their mindsets about school," Felke says. "We often see this professionalism appear in our students during presentation days when a majority of the students will choose to dress up."

Facility Overview

The Weidner School of Inquiry is a small, newly renovated learning community inside Plymouth High School, featuring:

- Six double classrooms meant to accommodate 50 students each.
- Three single classrooms.
- Three small technology infused collaboration rooms.
- Multiple flex spaces (5) with comfortable, moveable furniture to promote collaboration.
- A makerspace that promotes hands-on learning, used by science courses for classes Bio-Art, Chem-Food Science, and Physics-Sustainable Energy.
- Courtyard area located outside first floor annex (a permanent space with a flex area and 3 single classrooms); may be developed as a community garden or an outside collaboration area.

Teaching with Purpose

The Weidner School of Inquiry encourages educators to be more creative in their teaching through hands-on experimentation. They do so by facilitating collaboration among students, embracing the ideas of all students, personalizing instruction based on student needs, communicating expectations while allowing flexibility, and utilizing the strategies that best suit student success both academically and socially. The curriculum's relevance gives students a real-life connection to core subjects that, in turn, create authentic learning experiences that give meaning and purpose to what the students are learning.

"One of the most inspiring uses of our spaces was last fall during our sophomore's American Perspectives World War II project," Delp says. "They completed numerous interviews of WW II veterans that were videotaped and archived to preserve history. This experience was enriched by our flexible and inviting learning spaces. For other projects, we have a 3D printer in one of our three collaboration rooms where students who have expressed an interest in 3D printing use a 3D scanner to create models of manufacturer-requested prototypes."

Technology is, of course, an important aspect of building digital-age skills. The Weidner School of Inquiry uses technology as a tool to enhance the development of the skills necessary to prepare learners for meeting the demands of the workforce. Students manage their coursework with their own laptops, and the school's flex spaces include wall-mounted TV screens that students can plug into at anytime. These tools help to promote collaboration and provide opportunities for students to connect with the digital work of others.

"Transforming a learning space is about more than just furniture, but learning how the space can enhance and support the curriculum, targeted learning outcomes, or teaching methods," Felke explains. "At the Weidner School of Inquiry, the foundation has been laid for an amazing way to educate young people. We have an unparalleled learning space. We have a great mix of talented and dedicated facilitators who care very deeply for young people and their education. With hard work, purposeful collaboration, and constant communication, we hope that our small learning community will become a special place for the community, our staff, our facilitators, and most of all our learners, to all learn and grow together."

Digital-Age Skills Supported

- Critical Thinking and Problems Solving: Students are given the opportunity to learn through experimentation and exploration.
- Communication and Collaboration: Students collaborate with one another in groups and communicate with community leaders to discuss research.
- Technology Skills: All students have access to laptop computers, and can use digital screens and multimedia tools to collaborate with other students on projects.

Once fully implemented, one-third of the Plymouth High School population will receive their instruction of core classes (science, math, English, and social studies) in the Weidner School of Inquiry. Some of these courses are integrated with elective courses.

7

Planning for Active Learning Spaces

I f you've read this far in the book, you're probably already convinced that redesigned learning spaces benefit students and teachers. You've also probably generated some ideas for your own classroom or school, some that are pie in the sky and some more grounded in reality. Now it's time to think about the steps you can take to transform your learning environment into one that effectively uses space to engage students and enhance learning.

A solitary teacher with some ideas about how to reform one classroom to meet the needs of the digital age has the opportunity, with administrative support, to make significant changes in one small learning space. This may involve raising money for more flexible furniture, writing a grant to acquire technology, or just rethinking the classroom design. In many cases a small step, like the rethinking of one classroom space, can be an excellent strategy for moving a whole school forward. One redesigned classroom can be an example that inspires other teachers. It can also help a faculty work out the design kinks to facilitate a more widespread application of active learning spaces. Even if only one classroom is redesigned, it can at least improve the learning experiences of the students in that classroom.

Room 17

When Pamela Kennedy decided to design a flexible classroom environment that met the needs of her students, she explored a variety of funding options in order to purchase the special furniture and equipment she needed.

Ms. Kennedy has found success with DonorsChoose.org, a website that connects public school teachers and their projects with donors. Ms. Kennedy figured out how to ensure successful grant applications, and she focuses on specific regional grants and matching donations from corporations. She does this so as to avoid overburdening the financial resources of her school and local community. Now Ms. Kennedy is passing on her expertise in navigating the DonorsChoose.org site to her colleagues and other educators.

Get Active: Reimagining Learning Spaces for Student Success   **133**

ISTE Standards for Administrators

Effective adoption of teaching and learning best practices for both technology integration and a pedagogical shift to active learning requires knowledgeable, skillful, and inspiring administrators. The following ISTE Standards for Administrators (ISTE Standards•A) define the various roles administrators play in seizing opportunities to transform schools to fit the educational requirements of the digital age:

1. Visionary leadership
   Educational Administrators inspire and lead development and implementation of a shared vision for comprehensive integration of technology to promote excellence and support transformation throughout the organization.

2. Digital age learning culture
   Educational Administrators create, promote, and sustain a dynamic, digital-age learning culture that provides a rigorous, relevant, and engaging education for all students.

3. Excellence in professional practice
   Educational Administrators promote an environment of professional learning and innovation that empowers educators to enhance student learning through the infusion of contemporary technologies and digital resources.

4. Systemic improvement
   Educational Administrators provide digital age leadership and management to continuously improve the organization through the effective use of information and technology resources.

5. Digital citizenship
   Educational Administrators model and facilitate understanding of social, ethical and legal issues and responsibilities related to an evolving digital culture.

Visit www.iste.org/standards for additional resources and information about the ISTE Standards•A.

School leaders and administrators have the authority to take on bigger challenges, such as the building of a new school or significantly revamping an existing school to take advantage of what we know about how spaces can affect student learning. Making this dream a reality is a huge undertaking but is well worth the effort.

Before attempting the actual process of creating a redesigned learning environment, the school and community must be ready to make the most of the kinds of flexible learning spaces that support active learning. The most important component of readiness is the education and buy-in of teachers. They must be prepared to engage in student-centered approaches to instruction that seamlessly integrate technology into the learning process.

Engage and Educate Teachers

Active learning spaces only deliver on their educational promise when instruction moves toward student-centered approaches to teaching and learning. If there is no desire for a more collaborative and personalized pedagogy, then even the best designed physical environment will degenerate into a modern replica of the industrial age school. It will be a more attractive space but will not make much of a difference for students. Although sometimes a revolutionary physical environment can inspire teachers to make changes in their teaching methods, the opposite can also happen: Teachers arrange their moveable furniture in rows facing the "front" of a flexible space and leave it there; students access technology only to complete tests and worksheets; and exciting new digital and analog resources gather dust in storage rooms. The school may look different, but, fundamentally, nothing has really changed. And this would be a tragedy for all concerned, not to mention a huge waste of time and money!

Consequently, the biggest consideration when planning for redesigned learning spaces is professional development for teachers. Helping teachers think about learning differently is the right place to begin thinking about improving student learning, even before making a commitment to redesigned learning spaces. Student-centered instruction is a good thing, regardless of the learning environment, and transforming classroom pedagogy can benefit students even in traditional learning spaces. You lose nothing by focusing on helping teachers create more active learning experiences for students, and everyone benefits.

Teachers who are proficient at student-centered instruction have much to offer an educational community that is considering a redesigned school. Due to their experience, they will be invaluable resources for choosing plans and for adapting them to the specific needs of a school. Because they are also aware of the shortcomings of an existing environment, they will have creative ideas on how best to meet learning goals with the available spaces. By working with architects as well as other stakeholders in the planning process, experienced student-centered teachers can make sure that the final building will meet the unique needs of their school and community. They can easily transition into the new environment since they already use teaching practices that incorporate different physical arrangements. Finally, these expert teachers can also serve as ambassadors to teachers and other colleagues who are interested but apprehensive.

 **YOUR TURN**

Make a list of inspiring teachers in your school.

How might they each be able to contribute in preparing other teachers for the instructional shift to student-centered learning or in planning a school redesign project?

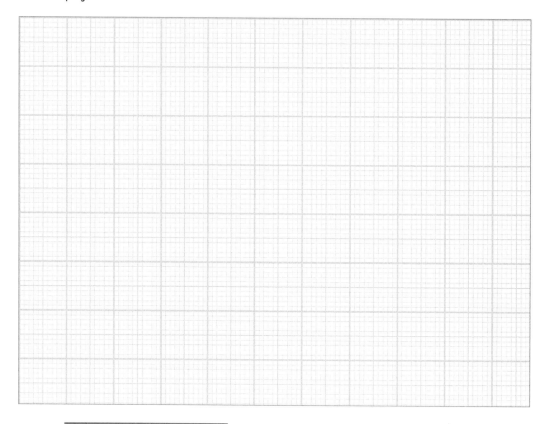

Researchers have been studying the types and effects of teacher learning experiences on teacher behaviors and student learning for many years. This research has identified several characteristics of high-quality professional development:

- It is focused on content.
- It is designed around how students learn.
- It provides in-depth, active learning opportunities.
- It links to high academic standards.
- It offers teachers opportunities to participate in leadership roles.
- It is of an extended duration.
- It encourages collaboration among groups of teachers (Desimone et al., 2002).

The effective use of technology is an important component of professional development that promotes active learning experiences that are supported by flexible digital-age school design. In a digital-age learning environment, students use technology to manage and personalize their learning. While technology is an important component of a digital-age learning environment, it only plays a role when it supports active learning.

Teachers who teach from a student-centered perspective can benefit from professional development that focuses on technology skills and practical teaching ideas. These teachers will take immediate advantage of learning spaces that support student-centered learning with technology. Less proficient teachers who are reluctant to implement active learning approaches to learning will need professional development that focuses as much on pedagogy as on technology.

Clearly, implementation of professional development that meets these criteria is a far cry from the hiring of an outside expert to talk to teachers about student-centered instruction or flexible learning spaces for an afternoon. Professional development requires considerable planning, funds, and effort. While professional development to help teachers learn how to develop active learning experiences for students can take place early in the process of a redesign project, additional teacher learning activities will have to be provided once the building is complete. Even teachers with experience in an active learning environment will need support to take full advantage of the new environment.

Still, the key to the success of a school design that supports flexibility and active, personalized learning lies in a commitment to educating teachers in ways that transform traditional industrial-based learning environments into places that prepare students for the digital-age world.

Puentedura's Stages of Technology Integration

Puentedura's model of technology integration describes a way of thinking about technology in the context of how it contributes to student learning. This model focuses on Substitution, Augmentation, Modification, and Redefinition (SAMR). Teacher professional development in SAMR can provide a framework and common vocabulary for how technology is used in the classroom, guiding teachers towards meaningful and impactful technology integrations.

- **Substitution:** Students use technology to complete traditional teacher-directed tasks, such as quizzes and worksheets.
- **Augmentation:** Students are still engaged in traditional teacher-centered learning activities, but the experience is somewhat enhanced through technology. For example, students may take a quiz online in order to progress to a new skill.
- **Modification:** Students use technology to complete tasks that they would normally have completed in another way, such as making a video instead of performing a live scene from a play.
- **Redefinition:** Technology opens up entirely new avenues for learning by allowing students to create and consume in ways impossible without technology (Puentedura, 2010).

ISTE Essential Condition: Ongoing Professional Learning

"Educators have ongoing access to technology-related professional learning plans and opportunities as well as dedicated time to practice and share ideas."

ISTE identifies professional learning that is continually implemented, up-to-date, and individualized as imperative to leveraging technology. This ongoing learning should include pedagogical best practices in active learning spaces as well.

 YOUR TURN

Rank professional development experiences you have planned or participated in by placing them on the line from least to most effective.

least effective   **most effective**

What has and hasn't worked in your experience?

What do you believe are the most important characteristics of effective professional development?

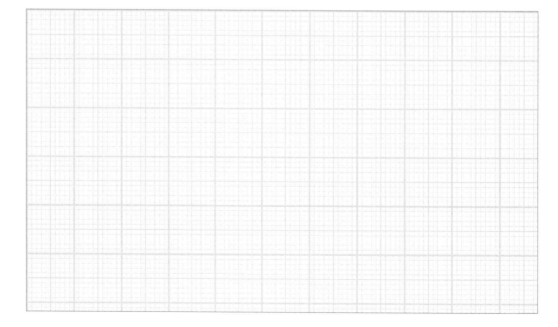

Steps to School Redesign

You must recognize that by proposing the construction of an active learning space you are proposing a radical change to the status quo. Your redesign will likely be a cause of concern for many, if not most, stakeholders. Before you begin thinking about construction, designs, furniture, and technology, you must first build a coalition of like-minded people to help move the vision forward. One person can make a difference, but a group of people can make more of a difference. Moreover, a support group can keep you going strong when challenges arise.

Leadership can begin anywhere, but the expense involved in building or redesigning a school means that district and school administrators have to be on board with the active learning spaces project. And their leadership has to go beyond allowing the vision to move forward. They must reflect the kind of revolution that active learning spaces bring, and become active collaborators who champion an inclusive process that systematically considers all options and decisions.

Form a Planning Committee

Any kind of school construction, whether it is building a brand-new school or updating an existing one, is an endeavor that requires significant community support. In most cases, such projects are subject to voter approval and, consequently, require community input throughout the planning and building process. But community participation isn't just a fiscal requirement when it comes to creating active learning spaces; it's a cultural, political, and social requirement as well. Well-designed spaces form a bridge between the school and the community, bringing community members into the school to play important roles in the learning process.

Individuals involved in planning for new or updated school construction may hold prior beliefs that restrict the ways they look at teaching and learning. These beliefs are often difficult to challenge and overcome, even with credible arguments:

- Stakeholders have tacit, deeply held beliefs about what schools are and what they should do.
- Parents, administrators, and many teachers have a bias toward traditional approaches to schooling, similar to the Ford model, and the ones they grew up with.
- Community members see the school as the main force in passing on cultural beliefs and norms (Building Futures, 2004).

Therefore, forming a committee where all these beliefs can be aired and addressed is critical for the success of creating a digital-age learning environment. The 21st Century School Fund recommends that a planning committee consisting of "parents, teachers, administrators, other school staff, including custodians or building specialists, students, representatives of local school management teams, neighborhood residents without school-aged children, representatives of community associations, and local business leaders" (2004, p. 22). Parents of students from student-centered classrooms can be excellent resources and can have a big impact on helping skeptical community members overcome their concerns.

Community member who serve on school committees, such as those that focus on facilities planning, generally spend hours of thankless work on projects that can sometimes be less than stimulating. It's tempting for school leaders to ask for volunteers and then settle for whoever shows up, or call upon the "usual suspects" who seem to play a role in all community-school interactions. For the kind of change implied by redesigning for active learning spaces, however, school leaders should be advised to go out of their way to recruit and maintain a diverse population of participants.

Most important, this planning committee is the school's link to the community at large. The individuals on this committee have more opportunities to communicate the excitement about how new learning spaces could transform learning for students to their constituent groups than do educators. When challenges arise during the process, as they undoubtedly will, the groundwork done in forming this committee can help overcome them.

 **YOUR TURN**

Make a list of possible members for a school design process. Include any leaders or practitioners at all levels, formal and informal, from the school or community.

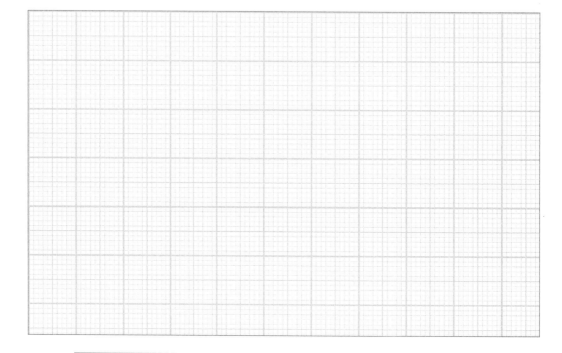

Conduct Research

Before the planning committee begins to discuss concrete ideas about what a school should look like, they need to take the time to collect some data that can help them make the right decisions about the school. Time is often a constraint here, so the committee needs to be systematic and organized about getting the information they need. One area of investigation would necessarily be the collection of information about the current state of the school that is being redesigned. In entirely new construction projects, information should be gleaned from existing or comparable schools to inform decision-making.

Longitudinal quantitative data on topics such as enrollment, class size, school demographics, graduation rates, and attendance can help focus the areas to be addressed in the process for redesigning existing structures and designing new schools.

Design Thinking and Active Learning Spaces

You may remember the concept of Design Thinking from Chapter 4: Redesigning Your Classroom. Reviewing the stages of Design Thinking may be useful when considering the process of planning a new or remodeled school.

- Empathize
- Define
- Ideate
- Prototype
- Test
(Stanford University Institute of Design, n.d.)

Survey data from stakeholders that include teachers, school staff, parents, and students can reveal general perceptions and trends. A well-designed survey gets input from people who don't have the time or inclination to participate in face-to-face meetings. Digital survey tools make this kind of information easy to collect, compile, and analyze.

Observations allow committee members to see how a school actually works, although they should certainly keep in mind that an observation on a specific day may not necessarily be typical. Because some people may tend to focus on particular behaviors, observing in teams can generate more reliable and unbiased findings.

Interviews with stakeholders can uncover the kind of in-depth information about attitudes and impressions that can't be learned from surveys or discussions. Using other kinds of data to help form questions can help to fill in knowledge gaps that, in turn, are needed to make good decisions. In addition, the ability to ask for further clarification about a statement and probing interesting comments for further elaboration can lead to a new level of understanding of the perspectives of people who play various roles in the school redesign process. Committee members must remember, however, not to overgeneralize from the comments of one or two interviewees. Rather, they must consider each idea in the context of all the data they have collected.

 **YOUR TURN**

Brainstorm ideas for survey questions to send out to your community. Even though you may not yet be in a position to send out a survey, think about what types of information will be needed. What are the specific needs of your community, and what insights can best guide a committee in its decision-making?

The goal of analyzing all this information is to learn as much as possible about the people who will be occupying the new space, what they need, and what they want. Although people often enjoy being interviewed and even observed, those collecting this kind of data must be careful to make sure that their role is clear—that they are just collecting information and that they are not evaluating teachers, students, or administrators. If responders don't feel comfortable being honest, then all the effort put into this kind of research is a waste of time, and any conclusions drawn from the work will not provide useful guidance for the creation of active learning spaces.

Many stakeholders have vested interests in maintaining the status quo, and others simply assume without reflection that a new or redesigned school will maintain the same approach to teaching and learning that they have always experienced. Because many of the members of the planning committee may have relatively little experience. with revolutionary learning spaces, conducting research can be a subtle way to introduce people to a new way of thinking about learning spaces. In addition, reading a book, as a committee, such as David Thornburg's *From the Campfire to the Holodeck*, or relevant articles or websites, the planning committee could initiate some important discussions about why we do school the way we do and what might we do differently. The References section of this book can point you to some valuable resources.

If possible, committee members should also visit schools where spaces are used in creative ways to enhance student learning. Before setting up a site visit, however, make sure that learning spaces are redesigned in more than superficial ways—that instruction is student-centered, and that students are doing creative and content-rich work. If students end up using collaborative groupings to memorize vocabulary words or accessing technology for drill and practice, fundamental assumptions about teaching and learning will not be challenged, and any new learning spaces will not bring about the changes in student engagement and learning that make this project worth the time, money, and effort.

As committee members participate in conducting research, collecting data, and sharing perspectives in open dialogue, they become educated to the reasons for the proposed changes to the learning environment. People will have a chance to air their concerns and

Researching Learning Spaces for Design39Campus

Design39Campus took research very seriously when designing their new school. The school district leadership took the principal out of the school two years to do research on school design before building the school. Five teachers were also given a year to network and conduct research about how space could have an impact on learning. They had thoughtful discussions about questions such as the following:

- Why is it that we're doing it this way?
- Why is it typically done this way?
- Is there a better way?

Community members and educators did additional research that included watching Ted Talks, reading books, and taking MOOC courses. Stakeholders considered all of this information when planning their new school.

objections, and the proponents of the changes will have the opportunity to refine and clarify their arguments for presentation to outside groups of stakeholders.

 YOUR TURN

Check the References section for possible resources to share with members of a committee. If time allows, create a presentation or summary of information you have discovered through your own research for committee members.

Create a Vision

The development of a shared vision for a school with learning spaces that meet digital-age needs has two purposes. First, the process of developing the vision is a bonding and focusing exercise for the planning committee. Although, at times, the haggling over wording and even over punctuation can be tedious and frustrating; eventually, the process should produce a clearly articulated statement that reflects the beliefs, goals, and compromises of a diverse committee—itself an important step in creating a revolutionary new school design. Second, a well-written vision statement serves as a vehicle for communicating with groups and individuals outside of the planning committee. Through formal and informal interactions with parent groups, teacher unions, local business associations, and architects and construction managers, committee members can use the vision statement to frame their comments and present a consistent view to all stakeholder groups and individuals.

ISTE Essential Condition: Shared Vision

"Proactive leadership develops a shared vision for educational technology among all education stakeholders, including teachers and support staff, school and district administrators, teacher educators, students, parents, and the community."

ISTE recognizes the importance of a community-wide vision in successful technology implementations. Establishing a shared vision about active learning spaces can similarly guide a school design process.

Plan

The actual planning of a school is a time-consuming process, particularly when the committee is working with revolutionary new concepts such as active learning spaces. At this point the process often seems overwhelming and can get rushed. Educators experienced at designing schools are often tempted to exclude input from the public in a desire to get the school built and meet deadlines (21st Century School Fund, 2004). But this is a big mistake, especially with a redesigned school that connects much more naturally with the community than does a traditional school. A school does more than affect student learning; it can also have an impact on a whole community. Glossing over concerns and issues at this stage diminishes the prospect that critical stakeholders will buy in to the whole redesigned learning spaces concept. And if that happens, you will end up with a beautiful building with the potential to transform learning that still processes students in a traditional cells-and-bells educational model.

Tools such as the construction of user scenarios or profiles can help committee members move their ideas forward. By taking on the role of a student, teacher, or other stakeholder, members of the planning committee can better anticipate needs and challenges. They can also consider the impact of various decisions on the people who will use the new space.

 **YOUR TURN**

Adopt roles of stakeholders in your community. Fill in the table while anticipating the perspectives that these stakeholders might have on a school design project.

Role of Stakeholder	Vision for Project	Needs	Challenges

Interview with an Architect

Carrie Perrone on Working with Schools to Design Active Learning Spaces

Carrie Perrone is a registered architect with SmithGroupJJR. Perrone, who serves as the firm's learning environments specialist, focuses on the planning and design of robust spaces for higher education, working with colleges and universities nationwide. As a member of SmithGroupJJR's Learning Practice Leadership, Perrone aims to bring the latest trends in design for engaged learning to today's academic institutions.

SmithGroupJJR has a long tradition of providing an integrated set of planning and design services that include campus master planning as well as programming and design for classrooms, laboratories, student-life facilities, libraries, professional schools, and specialized facilities. By taking the long view and designing for the whole campus, architects like Perrone have come to understand how space design affects an institution at room, building, neighborhood, and campus scales.

Setting the Stage for Active Learning

Perrone typically works with clients in the early phases of a project—pre-planning, programming, developing both building and "space" visions—then assigns the space list: the various components of a project. At the onset of a project, Perrone and her colleagues leverage benchmarking, past experiences, industry trends and data, relevant furniture solutions, tours, and impressions of peer facilities to help inform the project vision.

Through the visual listening process, Perrone guides discussions of a client's internal processes, organizes focus groups, and conducts discussion-based visioning exercises. "We begin a project by sitting with our clients and stakeholders, envisioning and listening: *truly* understanding how they do things, and getting a clear snapshot of a 'day in the life' of faculty, students, staff, and instructors," Perrone says. "We'll look at how and why they're doing things and work with them to design the right space for how the client needs to function." The outcome of this process is a client-specific vision that can be applied to the project at a programmatic level and carried through the design and completion of a new facility.

Learning styles and pedagogies become a primary focus when looking at formal learning spaces like classrooms or labs. They also factor into a study of informal learning spaces like study rooms or learning centers. It takes group input to understand what is needed in each type of space. From engaging technology and furniture consultants to working with faculty, administrators, and students to garner input, this process is critical to setting a framework for a successful active learning space.

Best Practices for a Successful Active Learning Spaces Project

Over the years, Perrone has developed a series of best practices for designing successful active learning spaces. These best practices help to ensure that new learning spaces are not just designed with custom furniture and technology but that the customization is specific to the larger goals of the institution.

Assign roles and seek out those invaluable project champions

Institutional leadership must be involved in the project in order for it to be successful. Engaging leadership that has a vision who can see that concept through implementation is critical. It is also extremely important to assemble the right steering committee to push the project goals forward.

"Success is about having the right people in mix," Perrone says. "If you have a naysayer, it's hard to get the ball moving forward. With active learning a steering committee needs to buy into the vision and really *own* that vision. A project's success is dependent on these strong voices and good decision-making. The architect's role is important, as we can provide guidance, leverage our expertise, and apply innovative design solutions. However, an engaged and empowered committee will make the project much more successful."

Get involved with the project. Have a voice.

The involvement of an organization's faculty, staff, students, technology consultants, and instructional experts is very important when designing active learning spaces.

"It's important to have conversations with all of the constituents," Perrone says. "We engage focus groups and talk to them about how they want to teach in the future and learn what their desired student outcomes are."

Understanding higher-level goals that the institution might have for curricula, research, and engagement enables SmithGroupJJR's planners to develop spaces that respond to specific goals set forth by the institution.

Research and benchmarking

Benchmarking gives clients valuable insight into industry trends, performance and size standards, and cost parameters associated with their project. Although every institution and facility is unique, benchmarking an educational facility in the context of similar peer facilities is a highly effective tool that allows for more informed decision-making.

Occasionally clients will do some benchmarking on their own, which can be extremely helpful. "When starting a project, it's really nice if the client has done some preliminary research. One client, for example, as the design process was starting, conducted

Continued on next page

Continued from previous page

significant internal research looking at peer institutions, research on student outcomes, and external factors relating to their specific programs. They considered questions like: What are employers looking for? What is affecting knowledge retention? And, what regulations and accreditation issues are changing that may impact curriculum material?"

In addition to an institution's own research, SmithGroupJJR has performed dozens of benchmarking studies on behalf of these clients in order to help them understand factors affecting their facility design. "We have databases and tools that allow us to provide space comparisons, pull room types from graphic libraries, and understand costs. Routine post-occupancy evaluations of our projects allow us to continuously refine and test the data against performance metrics and industry best practices," Perrone says. "In addition to our own projects, we tap into a wide range of publicly available benchmark information as well as site visits of projects completed by others."

Understand the goal of the space

SmithGroupJJR's active learning spaces typically vary from classroom and presentation spaces to collaborative areas, specialized labs, meeting rooms, and even lounges with couches and high-top café tables. Some spaces feature a variety of furniture types while others may have a more consistent selection of flexible furniture. Regardless, most every space SmithGroupJJR designs is flexible enough to support multiple pedagogies. The bottom line is this: One space does not fit all. Understanding the goals for the learning outcomes in the space helps dictate what type of active learning design is most appropriate.

"We like when a space can be flexible or adaptable to function at least three ways; however, determining the priority function is a must. A space may function one way best but adapt to two different functions well," Perrone says. "You must consider more than the furniture—a space is supported by its infrastructure including mechanical systems, lighting systems (artificial and natural), IT and audiovisual systems. The controllability and flexibility of these systems become constraints unless the budget is endless, and we all know that is never the case."

Develop feedback loops

As a project kicks off, SmithGroupJJR leverages different formats to capture feedback from various stakeholders—everything from social media to student focus groups. Feedback loops start at the beginning of a project where stakeholders are given the opportunity to express ideas in real time. The loops continue throughout the project until completion, at which time SmithGroupJJR performs a post-occupancy evaluation. SmithGroupJJR uses both qualitative and quantitative measures for these analyses and leverages post-occupancy information for benchmarking in future projects.

Develop

It is at this stage that, according to the 21st Century School Fund (2004), all the effort put into community involvement pays off. Building schools takes more than vision, time, and commitment—it takes money. The financing of a new building, furnishings, and technology always require the support and participation of taxpayers. Nonprofit, philanthropic, and community organizations can also be in a position to contribute financially to a plan that helps meet their needs in an educational setting.

Additional research may be necessary at this stage, along with conversations with teachers and students. Committee members and key stakeholders should also meet with architects and investigate their past work on schools, if possible, to determine if they actually understand the kind of learning environment you want to create. You will also want to learn about equipment and furniture that will make the learning spaces flexible and promote active learning. Companies that the school has worked with in the past may not provide the resources that will help teachers take advantage of the flexible spaces, meaning that new venders must be contacted and their products evaluated.

ISTE Essential Condition: Consistent and Adequate Funding

"Ongoing funding supports technology infrastructure, personnel, digital resources and staff development."

Proper funding of technology initiatives and redesigned learning spaces requires adequate funding beyond the initial money spent on infrastructure. Funding should provide for ongoing support of new programs including professional learning for staff.

School finance is a highly specialized area of expertise, and there are likely only a few people in a district with a deep understanding of the various ins and outs of putting together the money necessary for financing a new school or redesigning an existing school. However, as always, taking the time to appropriately educate committee members can make the implementation of the plan much easier.

Implement

When the actual construction of a school building begins, the role of the planning committee naturally changes. They will be less involved in the process as it progresses to interactions with architects and contractors. Still, committee members need to stay connected to the process in case major changes need to be made. Their role may be to reconfirm the vision for the school, to investigate additional forms of financing, or to get more feedback from those who will be using the school. They should also be responsible for planning a celebration when all the work pays off in a beautiful new or redesigned school with learning spaces that help the students of today and tomorrow reach their full potential!

Beginning before the school is occupied and for several months into the school year, teachers and other school staff will need continuing professional development in order to take full advantage of all the benefits of the new learning space. Building strong networks among educators, with collaborative planning time so that they can discuss issues and visit each other's classrooms if they like, will help them address challenges and create new routines and policies to help everyone get the most out of the new learning environment.

An Iterative Process

Clearly, in a task as complex as designing a school, the steps and stages occur over and over, alternating between the general (such as the whole-school architecture) and the specific (where to store the lunchroom furniture when lunch is over). A specific piece of the puzzle may also be addressed through multiple iterations of the process as new information is discovered, prototypes are developed, and feedback is solicited. The process doesn't end after the new school is built or the redesign project is completed. With a shared vision of what they want learning to look like in their school, all stakeholders, including students, educators, administrators, and parents, are responsible for continuing to identify problems and design solutions to fine tune and enhance their learning space.

The creation of digital-age learning spaces is a long-term commitment to today's young people and their future. Although technology and the workplace will doubtless continue to undergo rapid change that will require educators to continue to grow in skills and knowledge, the basic components of learning and teaching remain the same. Students must be given meaningful work that focuses on important content and digital-age skills in an environment that supports that work with relevant resources and flexible learning spaces that meet their individual and collaborative needs.

 REFLECT & DISCUSS

1. What is your role in accessing or creating effective professional development for yourself, for your school, or for district staff?

2. Recruiting committee members from diverse populations throughout the community can be a difficult task. How can you convince potential members about the importance of their participation?

3. Imagining a digital-age school with active learning spaces is pure fun, but seeing an actual project through from start to finish can be a long process. What challenges do you anticipate encountering? How might these obstacles be overcome?

CONCLUSION

The End ... Or Just the Beginning?

Veteran educators and administrators across the country have been talking about integrating technology into the classroom since the 1980's. But as society continues to evolve with the use of technology for efficiency and productivity, our school districts—sadly—often continue to struggle with this evolution. Education is the greatest advantage any individual can have in which to meet society head-on as a well-prepared and productive citizen. But when education doesn't include access to technology, can students truly feel prepared for college and career? If education happens within the four-walled confines of a traditional classroom environment—with its students lined up in rows and its teachers at the front of the class lecturing—is this adequately preparing students for lives and professions that will require creativity, collaboration and critical thinking skills?

Learning needs to get active!

Today's learners come to school more in tuned with technology than ever before, but their use of this technology is often personal and not typically used for the acquiring of new academic knowledge. They also realize that learning and working with peers can happen in any place and at any time. Classrooms of today should seize the opportunity to engage these digital natives and meet them where they are in their use of technology. These classrooms should also be flexible, physical spaces devoted to embracing the digital world while accommodating the many, unique ways that individual students *truly* learn. Teachers should use technology and space to amplify their ability to personalize learning for their students. It is incumbent upon us as educators to embrace this innovative way to design instruction and physical classroom spaces in order for our students to thrive and become better prepared for their world beyond school. The stakes are too high *not* to.

In each chapter of this book, you've read about the many ways educators and administrators just like you are designing dynamic learning environments that merge modern techniques such as blended, flipped, and personalized learning with active learning concepts. These engaging, real-world examples were designed to help you lead the charge for adopting active learning principles in your school or district. Hopefully you feel motivated and inspired to do just that! This book also incorporates the ISTE standards—standards developed by the International Society for Technology in Education that guide instructional practices in instructional technology around the world— to make the connection between the standard and the practice in each chapter.

If you think your district, school, classroom or teaching practice needs an active learning makeover, then hopefully *Get Active: Reimagining Learning Spaces for Student Success* has given you the goods to do great things.

Let the active learning spaces revolution begin!

—Kecia Ray, Ed. D.
Executive Director, Center for Digital Learning
Chair, ISTE Board of Directors 2012-2015

APPENDIX A
ISTE STANDARDS

ISTE Standards for Students (Standards•S)

All K-12 students should be prepared to meet the following standards and performance indicators.

1. **Creativity and Innovation**

   Students demonstrate creative thinking, construct knowledge, and develop innovative products and processes using technology. Students:

   a. apply existing knowledge to generate new ideas, products, or processes
   b. create original works as a means of personal or group expression
   c. use models and simulations to explore complex systems and issues
   d. identify trends and forecast possibilities

2. **Communication and Collaboration**

   Students use digital media and environments to communicate and work collaboratively, including at a distance, to support individual learning and contribute to the learning of others. Students:

   a. interact, collaborate, and publish with peers, experts, or others employing a variety of digital environments and media
   b. communicate information and ideas effectively to multiple audiences using a variety of media and formats
   c. develop cultural understanding and global awareness by engaging with learners of other cultures
   d. contribute to project teams to produce original works or solve problems

3.   Research and Information Fluency

Students apply digital tools to gather, evaluate, and use information. Students:

a.   plan strategies to guide inquiry

b.   locate, organize, analyze, evaluate, synthesize, and ethically use information from a variety of sources and media

c.   evaluate and select information sources and digital tools based on the appropriateness to specific tasks

d.   process data and report results

4.   Critical Thinking, Problem Solving, and Decision Making

Students use critical-thinking skills to plan and conduct research, manage projects, solve problems, and make informed decisions using appropriate digital tools and resources. Students:

a.   identify and define authentic problems and significant questions for investigation

b.   plan and manage activities to develop a solution or complete a project

c.   collect and analyze data to identify solutions and make informed decisions

d.   use multiple processes and diverse perspectives to explore alternative solutions

5.   Digital Citizenship

Students understand human, cultural, and societal issues related to technology and practice legal and ethical behavior. Students:

a.   advocate and practice the safe, legal, and responsible use of information and technology

b.   exhibit a positive attitude toward using technology that supports collaboration, learning, and productivity

c.   demonstrate personal responsibility for lifelong learning

d.   exhibit leadership for digital citizenship

6.   Technology Operations and Concepts

Students demonstrate a sound understanding of technology concepts, systems, and operations. Students:

a.   understand and use technology systems

b.   select and use applications effectively and productively

c.   troubleshoot systems and applications

d.   transfer current knowledge to the learning of new technologies

ISTE Standards for Teachers (Standards•T)

All classroom teachers should be prepared to meet the following standards and performance indicators.

1. **Facilitate and Inspire Student Learning and Creativity**

    Teachers use their knowledge of subject matter, teaching and learning, and technology to facilitate experiences that advance student learning, creativity, and innovation in both face-to-face and virtual environments. Teachers:

    a. promote, support, and model creative and innovative thinking and inventiveness

    b. engage students in exploring real-world issues and solving authentic problems using digital tools and resources

    c. promote student reflection using collaborative tools to reveal and clarify students' conceptual understanding and thinking, planning, and creative processes

    d. model collaborative knowledge construction by engaging in learning with students, colleagues, and others in face-to-face and virtual environments

2. **Design and Develop Digital-Age Learning Experiences and Assessments**

    Teachers design, develop, and evaluate authentic learning experiences and assessments incorporating contemporary tools and resources to maximize content learning in context and to develop the knowledge, skills, and attitudes identified in the ISTE Standards•S. Teachers:

    a. design or adapt relevant learning experiences that incorporate digital tools and resources to promote student learning and creativity

    b. develop technology-enriched learning environments that enable all students to pursue their individual curiosities and become active participants in setting their own educational goals, managing their own learning, and assessing their own progress

    c. customize and personalize learning activities to address students' diverse learning styles, working strategies, and abilities using digital tools and resources

    d. provide students with multiple and varied formative and summative assessments aligned with content and technology standards and use resulting data to inform learning and teaching

3. **Model Digital-Age Work and Learning**

    Teachers exhibit knowledge, skills, and work processes representative of an innovative professional in a global and digital society. Teachers:

    a. demonstrate fluency in technology systems and the transfer of current knowledge to new technologies and situations
    b. collaborate with students, peers, parents, and community members using digital tools and resources to support student success and innovation
    c. communicate relevant information and ideas effectively to students, parents, and peers using a variety of digital-age media and formats
    d. model and facilitate effective use of current and emerging digital tools to locate, analyze, evaluate, and use information resources to support research and learning

4. **Promote and Model Digital Citizenship and Responsibility**

    Teachers understand local and global societal issues and responsibilities in an evolving digital culture and exhibit legal and ethical behavior in their professional practices. Teachers:

    a. advocate, model, and teach safe, legal, and ethical use of digital information and technology, including respect for copyright, intellectual property, and the appropriate documentation of sources
    b. address the diverse needs of all learners by using learner-centered strategies and providing equitable access to appropriate digital tools and resources
    c. promote and model digital etiquette and responsible social interactions related to the use of technology and information
    d. develop and model cultural understanding and global awareness by engaging with colleagues and students of other cultures using digital-age communication and collaboration tools

5. **Engage in Professional Growth and Leadership**

    Teachers continuously improve their professional practice, model lifelong learning, and exhibit leadership in their school and professional community by promoting and demonstrating the effective use of digital tools and resources. Teachers:

    a. participate in local and global learning communities to explore creative applications of technology to improve student learning
    b. exhibit leadership by demonstrating a vision of technology infusion, participating in shared decision making and community building, and developing the leadership and technology skills of others

    c.   evaluate and reflect on current research and professional practice on a regular basis to make effective use of existing and emerging digital tools and resources in support of student learning

    d.   contribute to the effectiveness, vitality, and self-renewal of the teaching profession and of their school and community

ISTE Standards for Administrators (Standards•A)

All school administrators should be prepared to meet the following standards and performance indicators.

1. **Visionary Leadership**

   Educational Administrators inspire and lead development and implementation of a shared vision for comprehensive integration of technology to promote excellence and support transformation throughout the organization.

   Educational Administrators:

   a. inspire and facilitate among all stakeholders a shared vision of purposeful change that maximizes use of digital-age resources to meet and exceed learning goals, support effective instructional practice, and maximize performance of district and school leaders

   b. engage in an ongoing process to develop, implement, and communicate technology-infused strategic plans aligned with a shared vision

   c. advocate on local, state, and national levels for policies, programs, and funding to support implementation of a technology-infused vision and strategic plan

2. **Digital-Age Learning Culture**

   Educational Administrators create, promote, and sustain a dynamic, digital-age learning culture that provides a rigorous, relevant, and engaging education for all students. Educational Administrators:

   a. ensure instructional innovation focused on continuous improvement of digital-age learning

   b. model and promote the frequent and effective use of technology for learning

   c. provide learner-centered environments equipped with technology and learning resources to meet the individual, diverse needs of all learners

   d. ensure effective practice in the study of technology and its infusion across the curriculum

   e. promote and participate in local, national, and global learning communities that stimulate innovation, creativity, and digital-age collaboration

3. Excellence in Professional Practice

Educational Administrators promote an environment of professional learning and innovation that empowers educators to enhance student learning through the infusion of contemporary technologies and digital resources. Educational Administrators:

a. allocate time, resources, and access to ensure ongoing professional growth in technology fluency and integration

b. facilitate and participate in learning communities that stimulate, nurture, and support administrators, faculty, and staff in the study and use of technology

c. promote and model effective communication and collaboration among stakeholders using digital-age tools

d. stay abreast of educational research and emerging trends regarding effective use of technology and encourage evaluation of new technologies for their potential to improve student learning

4. Systemic Improvement

Educational Administrators provide digital-age leadership and management to continuously improve the organization through the effective use of information and technology resources. Educational Administrators:

a. lead purposeful change to maximize the achievement of learning goals through the appropriate use of technology and media-rich resources

b. collaborate to establish metrics, collect and analyze data, interpret results, and share findings to improve staff performance and student learning

c. recruit and retain highly competent personnel who use technology creatively and proficiently to advance academic and operational goals

d. establish and leverage strategic partnerships to support systemic improvement

e. establish and maintain a robust infrastructure for technology including integrated, interoperable technology systems to support management, operations, teaching, and learning

5. **Digital Citizenship**

Educational Administrators model and facilitate understanding of social, ethical, and legal issues and responsibilities related to an evolving digital culture. Educational Administrators:

a. ensure equitable access to appropriate digital tools and resources to meet the needs of all learners

b. promote, model, and establish policies for safe, legal, and ethical use of digital information and technology

c. promote and model responsible social interactions related to the use of technology and information

d. model and facilitate the development of a shared cultural understanding and involvement in global issues through the use of contemporary communication and collaboration tools

REFERENCES

21st Century School Fund. (2004). *For generations to come.* Retrieved from www.21csf
.org/csf-home/documents/organizing_manual.pdf

Barron, B. & Darling-Hammond, L. (2008). *Teaching for meaningful learning.*
San Francisco, CA: Jossey-Bass. Retrieved from www.edutopia.org/pdfs/
edutopia-teaching-for-meaningful-learning.pdfhttp://www.edutopia.org/pdfs/
edutopia-teaching-for-meaningful-learning.pdf

Benden, M.E., Zhao, H., Jeffrey, C., Wendel, M., & Blake, J. (2014). The evaluation of
the impact of a stand-biased desk on energy expenditures and physical activity for
elementary school students. International Journal of Environmental Research and
Public Health, vol. 11.

Bill, D. (2013, August 6). *8 tips and tricks to redesign your classroom. Edutopia.* Retrieved
from www.edutopia.org/blog/8-tips-and-tricks-redesign-your-classroom

Bretag, R. (2011, July 2). Evolution of the multidimensional learning space vision. [Web
log post] Retrieved from http://www.ryanbretag.com/blog/2011/07/evolution-of-the
-multidimensional-learning-space-vision/

Buck Institute of Education. (2010). What is project-based learning (PBL)? Retrieved
from bie.org/about/what_pbl

Building Futures. (2004). 21st century schools. Retrieved from www.dqionline.com/
downloads/cabe_21st_century_schools.pdf

Cannon Design. (2011). The third teacher+. Retrieved from www.thethirdteacherplus.com

Chua, J. (2007). Natural light gives you smartypants. Treehugger. Retrieved from www.
treehugger.com/culture/natural-light-gives-you-smartypants.html

Darling-Hammond, L., Zielezinski, M. B., & Goldman, S. (2014). Using technology to
support at-risk students' learning. Retrieved from edpolicy.stanford.edu/sites/default/
files/scope-pub-using-technology-report.pdf

Desimone, L., Porter, A., Garet, M., Yoon, K., & Birman, B. (2002). Effects of professional development on teachers' instruction: Results from a three-year longitudinal study. *Educational Evaluation and Policy Analysis,* 81–112.

Doorley, S. & Witthoft, S. (2012). *Make Space: How to Set the Stage for Creative Collaboration.* Hoboken, NJ: John Wily & Sons.

Drivers warned about loud muic. (2004, April 14). BBC News. Retrieved from http://news.bbc.co.uk/2/hi/uk_news/3623237.stm

Dunleavy, J. & Milton, P. (2009). What did you do in school today? Canadian Education Association. Retrieved from www.cea-ace.ca/sites/cea-ace.ca/files/cea-2009-wdydist-concept.pdf

edWeb. (Producer). (2015, February 25*). Designing Agile Learning Spaces* [Video webinar]. Retrieved from home.edweb.net/designing-agile-learning-spaces

edWeb. (Producer). (2015, February 17). *Makerspaces: The now revolution in school libraries* [Video webinar]. Retrieved from: http//home.edweb.net/makerspaces-now-revolution-school-libraries/

Gabrielson, C. (2013). *Tinkering: Kids learn by making stuff.* Sebastopol, CA: Maker Media.

Gallup, Inc. (2013). 21st century skills and the workplace. Retrieved from www.ferris.edu/HTMLS/administration/academicaffairs/extendedinternational/ccleadership/alliance/documents/Resources/21stCenturySkills.pdf

Hagel, J., Brown, J. S., & Davison, L. (2010, March 22). Three ways to distinguish an edge from a fringe. *Harvard Business Review.* Retrieved from: hbr.org/2010/03/three-ways-to-distinguish-an-e.html

Harris Poll. (2014). Pearson student mobile device survey 2014. Retrieved from www.pearsoned.com/wp-content/uploads/Pearson-K12-Student-Mobile-Device-Survey-050914-PUBLIC-Report.pdf

Hansraj, K. K. (2014). Assessment of stresses in the cervical spine caused by posture and position of the head. *Surgical Technology International, 25,* 277-9. Retrieved from https://cbsminnesota.files.wordpress.com/2014/11/spine-study.pdf

Hatch, Mark. (2013) *The maker movement manifesto: Rules for innovation in the new world of crafters, hackers, and tinkerers.* New York, NY: McGraw-Hill Education. Excerpted from Agency By Design. Retrieved from http://makingthinkinghappen.wordpress.com/what-were-reading/

Heppell, S. (2013, June 24). Rooms within rooms. Retrieved from rubble.heppell.net/rooms_in_rooms

Hilton, J. T. (2013). Digital critical dialogue: A process for implementing transformative discussion practices within online courses in higher education. *Journal of Online Learning and Teaching, 9* (4). Retrieved from jolt.merlot.org/vol9no4/hilton_1213.pdf

Horn, M., & Staker, H. (2011). The rise of K–12 blended learning: Profiles of emerging models. San Mateo, CA: Innosight Institute. Retrieved from www.christensen institute.org/wp-content/uploads/2013/04/The-rise-of-K-12-blended-learning.emerging-models.pdf

Intel Education. (Producer). (2015, February). *Intel teach live: How do we empower and inspire young women?* [Video webinar]. Retrieved from engage.intel.com/thread/23112

International Society for Technology in Education (ISTE). (2009). ISTE essential conditions. Retrieved from www.iste.org/standards/essential-conditions

International Society for Technology in Education (ISTE). (2015). ISTE standards. Retrieved from www.iste.org/standards

Jankowska, M. (2007). Use of creative space in enhancing students' engagement. *Innovations in Education and Teaching International, 45* (3), 271–79. Retrieved from www.beds.ac.uk/__data/assets/pdf_file/0019/11818/useofcreativelearningspaces.pdf

Khan, M. A. (2014, March 24). Teaching 21st century skills to ready students for the world of work. World Bank [Web log post]. Retrieved from blogs.worldbank.org/education/teaching-21st-century-skills-ready-students-world-work

Lai, E. (2011). Collaboration: A literature review. Pearson. Retrieved from images.pearson assessments.com/images/tmrs/Collaboration-Review.pdf

Lanier, J. (2014, November 12). The creation of SPMS Creative Commons [Web log post]. Retrieved from spmscreativecommons.blogspot.com

Lenhart, A. & Page, D. (2015). Teens, social media and technology overview 2015. Pew Research Center. Retrieved from www.pewinternet.org/files/2015/04/PI_Teensand Tech_Update2015_0409151.pdf

Lippman, P. C. (2010). Can the physical environment have an impact on the learning environment? JCJ Architecture, New York. Retrieved from www.oecd.org/education/innovation-education/centreforeffectivelearningenvironmentscele/46413458.pdf

Mahnke, F. (1996). *Color, environment, and human response: An interdisciplinary understanding of color and its use as a beneficial element in the design of the architectural environment.* New York, NY: Wiley.

McCrea, B. (2012). 6 ingredients for the 21st century classroom. *Campus Technology.* Retrieved from campustechnology.com/articles/2012/01/11/6-ingredients-for-the -21st-century-classroom.aspx

McCrea, B. (2012). Designing the 21st century classroom. THE Journal. Retrieved from thejournal.com/Articles/2012/01/18/Designing-the-21st-Century-K12-Classroom .aspx?Page=2

Mott, M., Robinson, D., Walden, A., Burnette, J., & Rutherford, A. (2012). Illuminating the effects of dynamic lighting on student learning. *Sage Open.* Retrieved from sgo.sagepub.com/content/2/2/2158244012445585

Nair, P., Fielding, R., & Lackney, J. (2013). *The language of school design: Design patterns for 21st century schools.* USA: DesignShare.

National Governors Association Center for Best Practices, Council of Chief State School Officers. (2010). *Common Core State Standards for mathematics.* Retrieved from www.corestandards.org/Math

Notosh. (2015). Design thinking: Ideation 1. Retrieved from notosh.com/lab/come-up -with-great-ideas

O'Malley, C. (Producer). Creadon, P. (Director). (2013). *If you build it* [Documentary]. USA: O'Malley Creadon Productions.

P21. (n.d.). 21st century learning environments. Slate. Retrieved from www.p21.org/ storage/documents/le_white_paper-1.pdf

Paul, A. M. (2013). You'll never learn! Retrieved from www.slate.com/articles/health_ and_science/science/2013/05/multitasking_while_studying_divided_attention_ and_technological_gadgets.html

Project Tomorrow. (2010). Unleashing the future: Educators "speak up" about the use of emerging technologies for learning. Retrieved from www.tomorrow.org/speakup/ pdfs/SU09Unleashingthefuture.pdf

Projects at High Tech High. (n. d.). The case of the cooties. Retrieved from http:// www.hightechhigh.org/projects/?name=Case%20of%20the%20Cooties&uid=fb b7713a028ce5ca4e2c8bd8b5b674bb

Puentedura, R. (2010). *SAMR and TPCK: Intro to advanced practice.* Retrieved from hippasus.com/resources/sweden2010/SAMR_TPCK_IntroToAdvancedPractice.pdf

Quinn, H., Schwengruber, H., & Keller, T. (2012). *A framework for K–12 science education.* Washington, DC: The National Academies Press.

Roshan, S. (2012, May 25). The flipped class: Students talk. Retrieved from www. thedailyriff.com/articles/students-talk-about-the-flipped-class-survey-results-933.php

Sköld, O. (2012). The effects of virtual space on learning: A literature review. *First Monday 17(1/2)*. Retrieved from firstmonday.org/ojs/index.php/fm/article/view/3496/3133

Sousa, D. (2012). *How the brain learns.* Newbury Park, CA: Corwin.

Stanford University Institute of Design. (2015). Retrieved from dschool.stanford.edu

Steelcase Education. (2013). Active learning spaces. Retrieved from www.k12blueprint.com/sites/default/files/active_learning_spaces_0.pdf

Steelcase Education. (2014). How classroom design affects student engagement. Retrieved from www.insidehighered.com/sites/default/server_files/files/Post%20Occupancy%20Whitepaper%20FINAL.pdf

Steelcase Education. (2014). Technology-empowered learning: Six spatial insights. Retrieved from www.steelcase.com/content/uploads/2015/02/Blended-Learning-Whitepaper.pdf

Taylor, L. & Parsons, J. (2011). Improving student engagement. *Current Issues in Education, 14*(1). Retrieved from cie.asu.edu/ojs/index.php/cieatasu/article/viewFile/745/162

Thomas, J. W. (2000). A review of research on project-based learning. Retrieved from www.bobpearlman.org/BestPractices/PBL_Research.pdf

Thornburg, D. (2014). *From the campfire to the holodeck.* San Francisco, CA: Jossey-Bass.

Vander Ark, T. (2015, February 21). Beyond the LMS: What next-gen learning platforms should do. Gettingsmart.com. Retrieved from gettingsmart.com/2015/02/beyond-lms-next-gen-learning-platforms

Warschauer, M. & Matuchniak, T. (2010). New technology and digital worlds: Analyzing evidence of equity in access, use, and outcomes. *Review of Research in Education, 34*(1), 179–225.

INDEX

metaphors for, 30
multidimensional, 123–124
for optimal learning experiences, 53–54
sharing, 82
spaces within, 52
student choice of, 65
student engagement and, 41–42
teacher research on, 65–66
types of, 30
libraries/media centers, 21–22, 98–99, 103, 112
life (learning space), 30
lighting, 61–62, 91–92
locker rooms, 99
lockers, 92
longitudinal quantitative data, 141
lunchrooms, 97, 108, 109

M
maker education, 101–104, 111–112
McGavock High School, 19
media centers, 21–22, 98–99, 103, 112
Mergendoller, John R., 32–33
Meriwether Lewis Elementary School, 81, 83–90, 97
metacognition, 82
metaphors for learning spaces, 30
Metropolitan Nashville Public Schools, 18–23
Microsoft Office 365, 122
mobile chairs, 45, 47, 58, 85
mobility, 57
multidimensional learning spaces, 123–124
music, 98, 109

N
National Assessment of Educational Progress (NAEP), 38
New Tech Network (NTN), 46, 127, 129. *See also* Weidner School of Inquiry
Node chairs, 45, 47, 85

O
observations, 141
Olson, Kenneth, 130
100 Ideas in 10 Minutes, 73
Orangewood Children's Foundation, 47–48
outdoor spaces, 92

P
P21, 16, 129–130
paper, building with, 102
parents, 78, 109
passive learning, 26–27
Perrone, Carrie, 146, 147, 148
Perry Meridian Middle School, 102, 103
personal supplies storage, 60
planning committees, 139–140
planning for active learning spaces
    about, 133–135
    development stage, 148–149
    implementation stage, 149

as iterative process, 149–150
planning committee, forming, 139–140
research, conducting, 141–144
school redesign, steps to, 139–145
setting stage for active learning, 146–148
teachers, engaging and educating, 135–138
vision, creating, 144
planning guides, 79
Plymouth High School, 126, 127, 131, 132. *See also* Weidner School of Inquiry
podiums, 86
Poway Unified District, 104, 105. *See also* Design39Campus
Power, Megan, 105, 106, 109, 114, 115
Preddy, Leslie, 102–103
preindustrial era schools, 10–11
presentation stations, 60–61
private/alone space, 30
private/together space, 30, 53–54
problem-based learning, 32–34
procedures/skills, planning and pre-teaching, 81
professional development, 135–138
project champions, 146
Project Tomorrow, 39
project-based learning, 32–34
Prototype stage (Design Thinking), 74, 106
public/alone space, 30
public/together space, 30
Puentedura's stages of technology integration, 137

Q
quiet work, 53

R
rapid prototyping, 74
Ray, Kecia, 19–20, 20–21, 23
reading areas, 53, 86–87
redesigning your classroom. *See also* Design Thinking
    challenges, overcoming, 77–78
    furniture, repurposing, 76–77
    leadership, buy-in from, 75, 77
    planning guide, 79
    process for, 69–75, 87–88
    steps to, 139–145
    student involvement in, 69, 75, 81
research, conducting, 141–144
Richland School District Two, 74, 75, 77
rituals, daily, 64, 88–90
roles, assigning, 146
Room 17, ix, 81, 83–90, 97
Roshan, Stacey, ix, 31
routines, 64, 88–90
rug area, 86

S
Saba, Anthony, ix, 43, 44, 46, 47, 48
safety and security, 96–97
SAMR (Substitution, Augmentation, Modification,